AF024

MASSIMILIANO AFIERO

AXIS FORCES 25

WW2 AXIS FORCES

The Axis Forces 025 - First edition March 2024 by Luca Cristini Editor for the brand Soldiershop
Cover & Art Design by soldiershop factory.   ISBN code: 9791255890959
Copyright © 2024 Luca Cristini Editore (BG) ITALY.   No part of this publication may be reproduced, stored in a retrieval system or transmitted by any form or by any means, electronic, recording or otherwise without the prior permission in writing from the publishers. The publisher remains to disposition of the possible having right for all the doubtful sources images or not identifies.
Visit www.soldiershop.com to read more about all our books and to buy them.

The Axis Forces number 25 – March 2024

Direction and editing: Via San Giorgio, 11 – 80021 AFRAGOLA (NA) -ITALY
Managing and Chief Editor: Massimiliano Afiero
Email: maxafiero@libero.it - **Website**: www.maxafiero.it

Contributors

Tomasz Borowski, Grégory Bouysse, Stefano Canavassi, Carlos Caballero Jurado, Rene Chavez, Gary Costello, Paolo Crippa, Carlo Cucut, Antonio Guerra, Lars Larsen, Christophe Leguérandais, Eduardo M. Gil Martínez, Michael D. Miller, Peter Mooney, Péter Mujzer, Ken Niewiarowicz, Erik Norling, Raphael Riccio, Marc Rikmenspoel, Guido Ronconi, Hugh Page Taylor, Charles Trang, Sergio Volpe

Editorial

As usual, we start this new editorial year late with the release of the first issue of our magazine. As always, we apologize to our readers. We hope it was worth the wait to finally see the new articles published. Our intent is always to attract your attention with new topics and above all to accompany the articles with new and interesting iconographic material, such as to capture the attention not only of Military History enthusiasts but also that of modeling and uniformology enthusiasts. We do our best, but we always welcome suggestions from you and reports on any themes and topics to be covered to improve our work and make our magazine a point of reference. Let us now analyze the contents of this new issue of the magazine. We begin with the second part of the long and interesting work on the use of the Hitlerjugend Division *on the Normandy front, in the initial phases of the bloody fighting that raged on French soil in the summer of 1944. Following is a new article dedicated to the French volunteers of the* LVF *engaged in the Eastern Front between 1943 and 1944. We then return to talking about the* Nordland Division, *on its use on the Baltic front in the summer of 1944. We close with the second battle of the Don in which* Italian units *were involved in December 1942 and January 1943. Always hoping to have met your interest in military history, I wish everyone happy reading and see you in the next issue.*

Massimiliano Afiero

The publication of The Axis Forces deals exclusively with subjects of a historical military nature and is not intended to promote any type of political ideology either present or past, as it also does not seek to exalt any type of political regime of the past century or any form of racism.

Contents

12.SS-Panzer-Division 'Hitlerjugend' Normandy Front, 2nd part	Pag. 3
The French Volunteer Legion on the Eastern Front, 1943-1944	Pag. 29
The 11th Nordland division and the defense of the Baltic countries	Pag. 49
The Italian Army in Russia, the Second Defensive Battle of the Don	Pag. 71

12.SS-Panzer-Division 'Hitlerjugend' Normandy Front

by Massimiliano Afiero – 2nd part

The *PzKpfw.IV* '646' in the Ardenne Abbey sector.

SS-Hscha. Hans Müller after the destruction of his Panzer '518', during a reconnaissance.

The commander of the Canadian vanguard at that point ordered his companies to stand in a defensive position north of Authie. At the same time, the *9.*, *10.* and *11.Kp.* of *SS-Pz.Gr.Rgt.25* and the two *Panzerkompanie 5.* and *6.* continued their attack on Buron and Gruchy. They were supported by the fire of *III.Artillerie-Abteilung*, directed by *SS-Stubaf*. Bartling from the tower of the Ardenne Abbey, but also from light and heavy infantry guns, mortars and heavy machine guns. Company A of the *North Nova Scotia Highlanders* was overwhelmed north of Authie. The attack on Buron instead met with greater resistance and when the German units approached the southern outskirts of the city, a heavy barrage, unleashed by Canadian artillery, hit them, causing losses among the panzers and the SS grenadiers. In the confusion of the battle, Canadian artillery also hit their own units. Some panzers retreated to the Ardenne Abbey. *SS-Ostubaf*. Kurt Meyer immediately ordered them to return to the attack to support the *Panzergrenadieren* in their attack on Buron.

Testimony of *SS-Sturmmann Vasold*: *"... We attacked Buron with the remaining panzers, continuing to be engaged in house-to-house fighting. Numerous prisoners were captured. Under the incessant fire of enemy heavy machine guns, we were forced to relinquish ground again to the enemy. There was no possibility of continuing, we had to retreat again, under the protection of one of our panzers ".*

A *Hitlerjugend PzKpfw.IV* on Normandy front, during first engagements in June 1944 (DW).

Hitlerjugend Schwimmwagen **during a reconnaissance.**

At around 15:00, *SS-Staf.* Meyer ordered the *I.* and *II.Bataillon* to prepare for the attack as soon as their respective troops on the left had reached the same line. *II.Bataillon* did not have the enemy directly in front, as the Allied units closest to its attack front were located in Anisy. However, the battalion was exposed to enemy fire on its left wing, from men of the *North Nova Scotia* and the 27th Armored Regiment. The right wing of the battalion was attacked by the *2nd Royal Ulster Regiment*, supported by the *East Riding Yeomanry* tanks, which attacked from Le Mesnil in the direction of Cambes. After the *III./25* and the panzers of the *5.* and *6.Pz.Kp.* had conquered Authie and were advancing on Buron, the *II./25* of *SS-Stubaf.* Scappini and the *7.Kompanie* joined the attack: on the right, the *7.Kompanie* led by *SS-Hstuf.* Karl-Heinz Schrott advanced, on his left the *5.Kp.* of *SS-Hstuf.* Kurt Kreilein and a little further back on the left was the *6.Kp.* of *SS-Hstuf.* Anton Tiray. The *8.(schwere) Kompanie*, under command of *SS-Hstuf.* Georg Breinlich had not yet arrived. The panzers under the command of *SS-Hstuf.* Heinrich

Bräcker, followed immediately behind in a spread out formation. The position of Saint Contest was conquered shortly after without great difficulty. *SS-Stubaf.* Scappini advanced with the lead platoon of the *7.Kompanie*, together with his aide, *SS-Ostuf.* Franz-Xaver Pfeffer and *SS-Hstuf.* Fritz Sedlazek, battalion medical officer. Scappini ordered a short pause to align the companies and as he scouted the terrain with the other officers, three Canadian tanks suddenly appeared. The SS officers immediately ran for cover, but by now they had been spotted, coming under enemy fire: *SS-Stubaf.* Scappini was seriously injured.

A *PzKpfw.IV* of 6./*SS-Pz.Rgt.12* and a grenadier.

SS-Hstuf. Hans Scappini.

A *PzKpfw.IV* on Normandy front, 1944.

The regimental commander, Kurt Meyer, who had arrived on the spot aboard a motorcycle to learn about the situation, ordered *SS-Hstuf.* Schrott to assume command of *II./SS-Pz.GR.25* and *SS-Ostuf.* Kurt Havemeister took his place in turn. The panzers following *7.Kp.* forced the three enemy tanks to retreat. The battalion advanced further conquering Malon and Galmanche without encountering too much resistance, thwarted only by Allied artillery fire. The *I.Bataillon* of *SS-Stubaf.* Hans Waldmüller, regrouped on the right of the *II.Bataillon.*, having as its first objective the attack against Anguerny, nine kilometers north of Caen. After the *II.* and *III./25* had eliminated the threat on the left flank, *I./25* began the attack at 16:15. On the right, the *1.Kp.* advanced, on the left the *2.*, and even further to the left the *3.Kp.* The attack was supported by elements of *8.Pz.Kp.*, led by *SS-Ostuf.* Hans Siegel. Five PzKpfw IVs had arrived just before the attack began.

SS-Ostuf. Hans Siegel.

A *PzKpfw.IV* with lateral protection (*Schürzen*).

In the foreground a destroyed *Sherman* and in the background grenadiers and a *PzKpfw.IV* of the *Hitlerjugend* engaged in combat (*Die Deutsche Wochenschau*).

The advance continued slowly towards the southern part of Cambes. After the *Panzergrenadieren* of the 1.Kompanie had reached a wooded area north of Cambes, together with those of 3.Kp., Sherman tanks appeared on the left of the village, in front of the 2.Kp. grenadiers, opening fire. In the shelter of the trees, the grenadiers were stalled in their advance and at the same time the fire of Allied artillery and mortars also struck the wooded area north of Cambes, which was soon joined by the fighter bombers. Testimony of *SS-Schütze* Emil Werner of 3.Kompanie: "... *The time came for the attack on Cambes. We were ordered to go ahead. We could see the village very well from our position. On reaching its outskirts we were greeted by the fire of the enemy infantry. We launched an attack on a church, where some enemy snipers had holed up. Shortly after, I saw the first comrade of my company, SS-Grenadier Rühl, fall. I turned towards him, he had been hit by a bullet in the head. The situation immediately became critical. My group commander was wounded in the arm and had to be evacuated. SS-Grenadier Grosse of Hamburg jumped behind me towards some bushes with his submachine gun pointed, shouting 'hands up!': Immediately after, two British soldiers came out with their hands raised. Grosse was later decorated with the Second Class Iron Cross for this action. Ustuf. Gschaider*[7] *approached me soon after and we both took cover behind an abandoned Wehrmacht truck under a tree. Ustuf. Gschaider then pointed to a house saying:* 'Werner, shoot at it!'. *As I opened fire, Gschaider was hit by an explosive bullet in his face. He could no longer speak and had to be evacuated. A few seconds later, Uscha. Hatzke yelled at me:* '... Let's go on!' .... ".

Hitlerjugend grenadiers storming enemy positions.

Hitlerjugend grenadiers with an MG-42.

The panzers of *8.Pz.Kp.* then began their attack: one of the tanks was left behind due to a mechanical problem, while the other four advanced from the west of Malon, identifying several enemy positions to the west of the wooded area north of Cambes. Testimony of *SS-Ostuf.* Siegel: "... *I was in the lead with my panzer. Stopping to be able to shoot became more and more risky. So, I went along the edge of the forest to be more sheltered. A shell exploded in the trees causing numerous branches to fall on my panzer, completely limiting my visibility. At the same time, two of my vehicles were moving behind me. Both were hit when they stopped to start opening fire ... The fourth panzer fell into a crater in the ground, getting stuck. Our panzers were put out of action even before they were really engaged in action ...* ". Meanwhile, the *Panzergrenadieren* had destroyed three Shermans with *Panzerfausts*. *SS-Sturmmann* Köpke of *1.Kompanie* destroyed two tanks, *SS-Sturmmann* Würfs of *I. Zug* destroyed another.

Hitlerjugend grenadiers move to assault enemy positions.

Hitlerjugend grenadier with a *Panzerfaust*, 1944.

A *Hitlerjugend* defensive position with an MG-42.

A report from *SS-Uscha*. Helmut Stöcker, a member of the *I. Zug* of the *Schwere Infanteriegeschütz Kompanie*, the heavy infantry gun company, which supported the attack of the *I./25*, testifies to the great determination with which the attack was conducted: "... *The attack was launched quickly by the infantry. Due to the short range of our guns, we had to advance with the infantry, who were attacking without armored support. Everywhere, there was a massive barrage that blocked our advance. We were ahead of Cambes, on open ground with our vehicles and guns. In order to allow the infantry to continue moving forward, our platoon moved forward towards Cambes. We had no other choice and would probably be routed within ten minutes. After having reached Cambes, we took up our positions in a ditch: we could hear the sound of tracks coming from the village. About fifty meters in front of us, a Sherman suddenly emerged from a side street. stopped at an intersection and sighted us and our guns. The turret of the tank turned towards us and before we knew what was happening, the first shot landed on us. We were saved by jumping to the left, in the shelter of a half-destroyed farm. The next shot fell among our guns and tow vehicles. We were also lucky because it was probably an anti-tank shell and not an explosive shell. Already loaded with our material, we didn't have any anti-tank weapons with us, but luckily an I./25 grenadier arrived with a Panzerfaust. Thanks to a well-aimed shot, the Sherman was hit and destroyed, thus blocking the main intersection in the village. We took the opportunity to go back on the positions of the I./25. Our guns were left on the outskirts of the village ".*

A *Hitlerjugend* grenadier inspect a destroyed *Sherman* on Normandy front.

A *schwere Infanterie Geschütz 33* of *SS-Pz.Gren.Rgt.25.*

A *Hitlerjugend* soldier wounded in the face and bandaged.

The units of the *Ulster Rifles* came under fire from German artillery and mortars as they attempted to pass through the village of Le Mesnil and were eventually forced to retreat. The *I. Bataillon* could not pursue the enemy who was in retreat, and also because the whole wooded area was subjected to a massive barrage by the Allied artillery and mortars. An advanced observer of the *7.Batterie* accompanying the *I. Bataillon* was killed. His radio was destroyed, and artillery support was lost. The neighboring units on the right of *Panzer Regiment 22* of *21.Pz.Div.* had not yet grouped together so the right flank of the battalion was left uncovered. Given the situation, *SS-Stubaf.* Waldmüller decided to stop the attack, to disengage from the enemy and settle on defensive positions on the southern side of Cambes. The retreat took place smoothly, with companies entrenching themselves along a line running from the railway embankment west of La Bujude. Contact was established with *Panzer Regiment* 22 on the right and with the *II./25* on the left.

SS-Stubaf. Hans Waldmüller in the field south of Cambes, on the right, scans the horizon with other SS officers to decide the next moves (*Hubert Meyer Collection*).

SS-Hstuf. Willi Klein, on Normandy front.

The new positions were immediately subjected to bombardment by Allied artillery. Due to the non-arrival of the other divisions of the division, the left flank of *SS-Pz.Gr.Rgt.25* continued to remain uncovered. At around 16:00, the *Divisionbegleitkompanie*, the divisional escort company, under the orders of *SS-Ostuf.* Fritz Guntrum, in position to defend the divisional command post in Venoix, was ordered to go and check to see if the bridge over the River Mue in Rots had already been captured by the enemy. Shortly thereafter, two groups of the company entered Rots from the east and south, both coming under enemy fire, a sign that the position had already been occupied by the enemy. West of the River Mue, the enemy had already reached or crossed the Caen-Bayeux road. On the right of *SS-Pz.Gr.Rgt.25*, the *21.Panzer-Division* had not yet started its attack and until new reinforcements arrived, *SS-Staf.* Meyer ordered any further advance to be blocked. From one of the two towers of the Ardenne Abbey, he had spotted enemy tanks approaching Bretteville-l'Orgeilleuse from the north and west of the crest of Mue, a serious threat to his exposed left flank.

Hitlerjugend **grenadiers during an attack, June 1944** (*Michael Cremin Collection*).

SS Grenadiers in the courtyard of the Abbey of Ardenne.

The *I./25* therefore had to move south of Cambes while an armored counterattack on Buron was underway. At the same time, the Canadian 9th Infantry Brigade ordered the *North Nova Scotia Highlanders* to recapture Le Buissons. According to the report of the members of *SS-Pz.Rgt.12* and those of *III./25*, panzers and grenadiers launched a counterattack at the same time, occupying Buron and forcing the Canadians to retreat. *5.Pz.Kp.* led by *SS-Ostuf*. Helmut Bando, secured the northern side of Gruchy. When the order to stop the attack and go on the defensive was

A *Hitlerjugend PzKpfw.IV* on Normandy front (*Tiquet*).

SS Grenadiers in the courtyard of the Abbey of Ardenne.

Hitlerjugend grenadiers in a French village, June 1944.

given to the *II./25*, things did not go as planned. The battalion was sure that it would not encounter too much resistance in front of it and it was correct: the companies entrenched themselves on a curved line, around the position of Galmanche, while the battalion command post was installed in Malon. When night fell, scouting patrols were sent out to find out what the enemy was doing. On the morning of 7 June, *SS-Pz.Gr.Rgt.25* was therefore set up in defensive positions along a line that went from the Caen-Luc sur Mer train station to Route Nationale 13. The right wing of the *I.Bataillon* was located along the railway line south of Cambes, where a tenuous connection with the *21.Panzer-Division* had been established.

In the *II.Bataillon* sector, the defensive line ran on the left along the northern part of Galmanche, continuing along the northern part of St. Contest in the *III.Bataillon* sector, then along the northern and western part of Buron, until reaching the western area of Gruchy, Authie and Franqueville. *SS-Pz.Gr. Rgt. 25* had managed to repel the attack of the British and Canadians, blocking them north and northwest of Caen, also managing to repel the forward armored units that had pushed as far as the airfield at Carpiquet, inflicting heavy losses on the enemy. German losses were also considerable, mainly due to enemy artillery fire. The greatest enemy losses were recorded in the Buron-Authie-Franqueville area. *North Nova Scotia* alone reported the loss of 242 men, including wounded and killed, 21 tanks destroyed and another 7 damaged. The companies of *SS-Pz.Rgt.12* (5. and *6.Pz.Kp.*) located on the left flank, had lost a total of nine *PzKpfw IV* and other damaged tanks.

Left, the *PzKpfw.IV* '536' brought back to the rear after being damaged during the fighting on 7 June. Right, a young grenadier of the *Hitlerjugend* decorated with the Iron Cross.

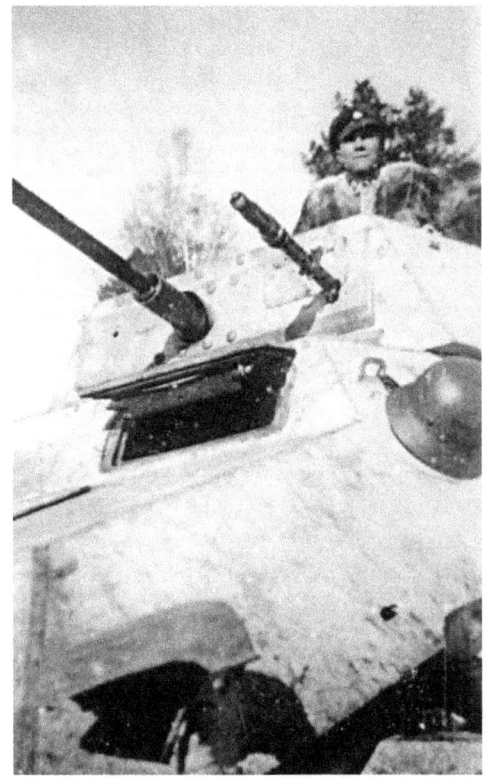

A *Sd.Kfz.232* of the *SS-Pz.Aufkl.Abt.12*.

The action of SS-Pz.Aufkl.Abt.12

While *SS-Pz.Gr.Rgt.25* fought north and northwest of Caen, *SS-Pz.Aufkl.Abt.12* was initially engaged further west, against units of the British 50th Northumbrian Division. When the leading units of the British 69th Brigade got to within about a kilometer of the Caen-Bayeux road, they met no resistance. It was not until the night between 6 and 7 June, that elements of *SS-Pz.Aufkl.Abt.12* reached the southern part of Caen and the Verson area, seven kilometers southwest of the city. As soon as dawn broke, the recon patrols went into action: one, equipped with an eight-wheeled armored car, sent in a northwest direction, collided with Allied units on the outskirts and near the Bretteville-L'Orgeilleuse railway station towards twelve o'clock. Another patrol, also in eight-wheeled vehicles, sent to the northwest of Caen, disappeared completely into thin air. An armored patrol of the *2.Kompanie*, in half-tracks, coming from Le Mesnil and led by *SS-Oscha*. Karl Jura, intercepted some Canadian jeeps south of Pûtot, then turned southwest. At Cristot, where the *Abteilung* command post was, he received the order at around 3:00 pm to carry out a reconnaissance in a northwest direction towards the sector of Seoul beyond Route Nationale 13, from Caen to Bayeux. After reaching the Seulles River near Tilly-sur-Seulles, *SS-Oscha*. Jura continued in the direction of Chouain and Ducy. In the latter location, enemy units, elements of the Durham Light Infantry, were encountered for the first time and were driven back.

A *Hitlerjugend Steyr 1500A* vehicle destroyed during an Allied air raid in Normandy.

Hitlerjugend half-tracks in Normandy, 1944.

The bulk of *SS-Pz.Aufkl.Abt.12* continued its march towards Tilly-sur-Seulles in the morning of 7 June. Attacks by Allied fighter bombers slowed the advance of the SS scouts, whose columns were hit hard. North of Cristot, a British light reconnaissance vehicle was destroyed. In Audrieu, an isolated infantry unit was intercepted and immediately put out of action: about twenty survivors were taken prisoner. An attack by the point company, moving north from Audrieu, met strong resistance on the outskirts of the city and was subjected to massive barrage by enemy artillery. The company took up positions on the western side of the position and was reinforced by a 75mm anti-tank gun and a platoon of light infantry guns. At that moment, the bulk of the *Abteilung* was still advancing along the Le Mesnil Patry-Cristot road, being attacked by an isolated British reconnaissance vehicle, which was soon destroyed by an anti-tank gun. The *Abteilung* then assumed a defensive position by preparing a series of fortified points, on a line that extended from La Rue (southeast of Audrieu), passed through the northern part of Audrieu to the area west of Hill 103. (southwest of Audrieu).

Motorized units of *SS-Pz.Gren.Rgt.26* on the march.(*Michael /Cremin collection*)

Hitlerjugend **grenadiers during an attack.**

The assembly and attack of SS-Pz.Gr.Rgt.26

While *SS-Pz.Gr.Rgt.25* and *SS-Pz.Aufkl.Abt.12* were already engaged in battle, *SS-Pz.Gr.Rgt.26* of *SS-Ostubaf.* Mohnke was still on its way to its assembly area, near Fontaine-Etoupefour. The units moved mainly during the day, suffering the attacks by Allied aviation in the afternoon of 6 June. The next day, these were even more intense, thanks to the improvement of weather conditions. The march then resumed dividing the units into small groups, widely spaced, to minimize losses. In the afternoon of June 7, the *I./26* reached Grainville-sur-Odon, southwest of Caen, immediately north of Route Nationale

175, which ran from Caen to Villers Bocage. A motorized patrol from the *1.Kompanie*, under the leadership of *SS-Oscha*. Friedrich Hahn, established connection with *Pz.-Lehr-Division*: south of the Caen-Bayeux road, the same patrol collided with some enemy elements, reporting losses. The battalion was ordered to regroup at Cheux, for an attack planned for the next day: the *3.Kompanie* was sent first to the area to secure it.

Hitlerjugend grenadiers during an attack under enemy fire.

A SS machine gunner.

SS-Stubaf. Bernhard Krause (BDC).

As the day progressed, the other regimental units also arrived in the area, while the Allies were driven back north and northwest of Caen, with heavy casualties. *SS-Pz.Gr.Rgt.26* had therefore received the order to attack on June 8, when it was still dark, with the support of *I./SS-Pz.Rgt.12* and *II./SS -Art. Rgt. 12*. However, the *Panzer Abteilung* did not arrive before the attack began, so that the regiment attacked without armored support. The plan of attack provided that *I. Bataillon*, under the orders of *SS-Stubaf*. Krause, were to conquer the position of Norrey and *II.Bataillon*, under *SS-Stubaf*. Siebken, that of Putot, as first objectives. *III.Bataillon*, led by *SS-Stubaf*. Olboeter, had the mission to secure the left flank and follow the attack behind *II.Bataillon*. The attack by the *I./26* began on June 8, around 3:00 am: the *3.Kompanie* under *SS-Ostuf*. Karl Düvel, was busy on the right, the *2.Kompanie* of *SS-Ostuf*. Siegfried Gröschel, on the left and the *1.Kompanie* commanded by *SS-Hstuf*. Helmut Eggert followed to the right to secure the flank. When the *3./26* reached the hill at St. Manvieu, it came under fire from some advanced Allied units, which immediately retreated towards Norrey. The *2./26* on the left initially advanced rapidly, then one platoon got stuck near the railway line, while the other two managed to seize the village of Cardonville, along the railway line. With the *3./26* stalled further back, *SS-Stubaf.* Krause ordered the suspension of the attack. The company in the meantime had settled in a defensive position: during the morning, *SS-Ostuf.* Düvel was injured as he moved between the positions of his men, then command of the company passed to *SS-Oscha.* Kaiser. The *1./26* which advanced to the right of the *3./26*, was also blocked shortly after, after coming under the fire of Allied artillery. The *II./26* had gathered during the night between 7 and 8 June, in the area of Le Mesnil-Patry. The first target of the battalion's attack was the village of Putot-en-Bessin, about a kilometer and a half north of Le Mesnil.

SS-Art.Rgt.12 **artillerymen busy transporting ammunition, passing near the carcass of a destroyed** *Sherman* **tank, partially visible on the left, Normandy front, June 1944.**

A *Hitlerjugend* **defensive position with an MG-42.**

The *Royal Winnipeg Rifles* were defending the village. At around 6:30 am, a recon patrol of *II./26* made contact with the Allied forces, when it attempted to enter the village by crossing the railway line and was driven back. The battalion then prepared for the attack with the *7.Kp.* of *SS-Ustuf.* August Henne on the right and the *6.Kp.* of *SS-Ostuf.* Heinz Schmolke, on the left.

A *Hitlerjugend* grenadier during an attack under enemy fire, June 1944.

Hitlerjugend grenadier.

Testimony of *SS-Ostuf*. Schmolke: "... our first target of the attack was the Caen-Bayeux railway line and the second, the Caen-Bayeux road. My lead platoon took prisoners. There was no time to question them, so we sent them directly towards the rear. An infantry platoon of the Panzer-Lehr-Division was attached to my company and participated in the attack. Shortly after I met with a Hauptmann, a battery commander, who supported our attack."

SS-Oscha. Paul Dargel, commander of the *III.Zug* of the 6.*Kompanie*, recalls the continuation of the attack: "... our first target was the railway embankment. The fire of the heavy artillery and the individual weapons of the enemy fell upon us. My platoon was engaged in the sector on the left of the road and the underpass. Our II.Zug was the first to reach the embankment. At 14:00 a message arrived: the company commander Schmolke was injured by shrapnel in the back. . ".

Thanks to the cooperation between all of the companies of the battalion, with the 7.*Kp.* of *SS-Ostuf*. August Henne engaged in clashes within the city, the Canadian units were completely surrounded inside Putot just after noon. Once they ran out of ammunition, they tried to retreat under the cover of an artificial fog, but only a few men managed to return to friendly lines.

A *Hitlerjugend* grenadier armed with a Mauser rifle fires at enemy infantry in the shelter of a hedge in the area north of Caen. (US NARA)

Hitlerjugend scouts committed to identifying enemy positions on Normandy front, June 1944.

When part of *6./26* reached its second objective, the national road, to its left, the open flank was attacked by numerous Allied tanks. *SS-Oscha*. Dargel observed at least 18 tanks of the 24th Lancers approaching: when they reached Route Nationale 13, they came under anti-tank fire east of St. Leger and this blocked their advance. In the afternoon the Lancers returned to the attack, meeting strong resistance west of Putot to the point of believing they were facing at least three battalions of the *Hitlerjugend*! At 8pm, the 7th Canadian Infantry Brigade launched a counterattack to try to regain lost positions in Putot, with the 1st Battalion The Canadian Scottish Regiment, reinforced by a company of the 6th Armoured

A well-camouflaged *Hitlerjugend Sd.Kfz.250* to escape Allied aerial reconnaissance, June 1944.

A *Sherman* of the 24th Lancers in Normandy bocage.

Regiment and some artillery batteries. Preceded by a massive barrage, the Canadian infantry and tanks attacked: the SS grenadiers tried to oppose them as best they could, but eventually had to retreat. The *6.Kp.* suffered heavy losses after an attack on the flank by the British tanks: the company commander together with a platoon leader after being wounded in combat, were captured by the enemy. Even the *5.* and *7.Kp.*, without adequate anti-tank weapons, were forced to retreat towards the railway line. Putot was recaptured by the Allies at 21:30. The *III. (Gep)./SS-Pz.Gr.Rgt.26* reached Fontenay-le-Pesnel, around midnight on 7 June, with the *10.Kp.* of *Oberleutnant* Wilhelm Pallas in the lead. The battalion was initially supposed to group on the left behind *II./26*, to secure the left flank of the regiment, and then follow *II./26* in its attack. Subsequently, the battalion was ordered to attack on the left of *II./26*, conquer Brouay and close the breach between *II./26* and *SS-Pz.Aufkl.Abt.12*. After marching on foot, the SS grenadiers reached Cristot at dawn on 8 June. The half-tracks were left in Fontenay and the panzers had not yet arrived. The battalion commander, *SS-Stubaf.* Erich Olboeter, had called a meeting with his company commanders in the wooded area five hundred meters north of Cristot. But the group of officers came under violent fire from Allied artillery and *Ostufs.* Pallas and Hauser were seriously injured. *SS-Ustuf.* Helmuth Mader, although wounded, then

The Axis Forces

A *Waffen-SS* mortar in a trench on Normandy front.

Soldiers of the *21.Panzer Division* engaged in combat along the Orne River, June 1944.

assumed command of *10.Kp.* and *SS-Ustuf.* Karl Kugler, that of *11.Kp.* Both companies were ordered to advance in the direction of Brouay, supported by the half-tracks, to capture the city and remain in its defense. The rest of the battalion was to remain in Cristot instead. The companies regrouped for the attack around 8:00 am. The advanced platoon of the *11.Kompanie* advanced east of the Cristot-Brouay road through a cornfield; about five hundred meters north of the city, the SS grenadiers came under fire from an Allied machine gun and only after silencing it, was the advance able to continue. Without firing a single shot, the suburbs of the city and the railway embankment were taken; with great surprise, some elements of the *Pz.-Lehr-Division* were cut off from the rest of their unit. The *10.Kp.*, advancing on the left of *11.Kp.*, despite the barrage unleashed by the Allied artillery, reached the wooded area southwest of Brouay. Some Allied tanks approached the railway line from the Loucelles area, but were repelled by the fire of the *10.Kompanie* mortars.

New attacks on Bretteville and Norrey

The units of *21.Panzer-Division* were in position on both banks of the Orne River, with those of *SS-Pz.Gr.Rgt.25* on their left. *II./SS-Pz.Rgt.12* and *Pz.-Lehr-Div.* received the order to head towards Bayeux, but first an attack had to be launched by *SS-Pz.Gr.Rgt.26*, with a limited objective. This attack was necessary for two reasons, first of all it was necessary to go and

A group of German Panthers before the attack, June 1944.

A self-propelled gun *'Wespe'* with SS grenadiers on board.

ascertain the defenses of the radar station at Douvres and at the same time, there was the possibility of splitting the Anglo-Canadian bridgehead in two. Before that, however, it was necessary to occupy good positions from which to launch the attack, some villages along the national road, such as Norrey and Bretteville-l'Orgeilleuse, at the same time establishing contact between the units of the two grenadier regiments of the *Hitlerjugend*. The divisional commander had ordered an attack for the night between 8 and 9 June on Bretteville by the Panther companies of *I.Pz.Abteilung*. However, only two of the latter's companies had arrived and were ready for use: the *1.Pz.Kp.* of *SS-Hstuf.* Berlin[12] and the *4.Pz.Kp.* of *SS-Hstuf.* Hans Pfeiffer. There were also the *15. (Krad.Kp.)/25* under the orders of *SS-Hstuf.* Horst von Büttner and the *2.(Sfl.)/SS-Pz.Art.Rgt.12* (equipped with self-propelled Wespen) of *SS-Ostuf.* Werner Timmerbeil. In command of the *Kampfgruppe* thus formed was *SS-Staf.* Kurt Meyer himself. Also, *SS-Ostubaf.* Max Wünsche, commander of *SS-Pz.Rgt.12*, joined the himself placed himself in command attack, although the staff of *I.Pz.Abteilung* had not yet arrived. As soon as it got dark, the *Kampfgruppe* began the attack, moving from the area south of Franqueville. *4.Pz.Kp.*

moved to the right of the road and *1.Pz.Kp.* on the left. Numerous motorcycle riflemen had boarded the panzers. *SS-Staf.* Meyer accompanied the troops aboard a sidecar of the *15.Kompanie*.

SS-Ostubaf. **Max Wünsche** aboard a *Panther*. (US NARA)

SS-Ostubaf. **Kurt Meyer.**

SS-Hstuf. **Hans Pfeiffer.**

The Panthers advanced at full speed towards their objective, while Meyer entered a small village on his motorcycle. The first group of motorcycle riflemen got off the motorcycles and the panzers and advanced on foot towards the bridge over the River Mue: the position was free from Allied forces and the bridge over the river was still intact. A few minutes later, the panzers also arrived. After crossing the bridge, they regrouped for the attack on Bretteville. *4.Pz.Kp.* continued advancing along both sides of the road leading to the village, with *SS-Hstuf.* Hans Pfeiffer in the second panzer. At one point, the tanks stopped a few hundred meters from Bretteville, taking up positions on a small elevation in the terrain. Fire from machine guns and Allied anti-tank guns began to hit them. Both Panther companies then concentrated their fire on the village entrance, supported by the 2nd Battery of the Artillery Regiment. When the panzers in the lead reached the entrance of the village, they fell under heavy fire from Allied anti-tank guns: Pfeiffer's Panther was hit and began to catch fire. *SS-Ostubaf.* Wünsche ordered *1.Pz.Kp.* to go around the village on the left and enter the village from the southwest, to renew the attack along the main road. Without adequate infantry in support, Meyer and Wünsche made the decision to stop the attack: for unknown reasons, the 2. and *3.Kp.* of *I./26* failed to exploit the attack of the panzers and the motorcycle riflemen on Bretteville.

The *Panther* '418' of the *SS-Uscha*. **Mühlhausen destroyed in Bretteville near a farm, headquarters of the *Regina Rifles Regiment*. The tank had been blocked by the explosion of mines which had damaged its right track (IWM).**

The *1./26* of *SS-Hstuf.* Helmut Eggert, on its own, managed to recapture Rots. Some Panthers from *4.Pz.Kp.* took up ambush positions on the outskirts of Bretteville. Since in the meantime a large gap had been created between the *I./26* and the two companies of the *I./26* south of Norrey, to close it and to ensure control of the road bridge over the River Mue near Le Bourg, the *Divisionbegleitkompanie* was ordered to join *1./26*. On that same day of 9 June, *Panzergruppe West* ordered *Hitlerjugend* to make a night attack with the aim of conquering Norrey, defended by strong enemy units. The mission was given to *3./SS-Pz.Rgt.12*, including twelve Panther tanks, under the orders of *Hauptmann* Lüdemann[14], without infantry and artillery support, hoping that the surprise effect would weaken the enemy. The German tanks advanced across the open fields towards their target when they began to be hit by the fire of the Canadian tanks, well stationed and hidden from their sight. One after another, the Panthers caught fire and together with them burned most of the crews. Six of the twelve Panthers involved were destroyed and the others had to fall back with serious damage. The Canadian infantry used machine guns to mow down the few survivors who tried to escape from that hell of fire and flames.

Panther tanks on the Normandy front waiting to attack, June 1944.

Hitlerjugend pioneers committed to building new defensive positions, June 1944.

The attack proved to be a total failure and, even more serious for *Hitlerjugend*, it left a Canadian fortified position wedged to the south, between the positions of *SS-Pz.Gr.Rgt.25* and *SS-Pz.Gr.Rgt .26*.

The attack of the pioneers

During the night between 10 and 11 June, the division's pioneer battalion, under the orders of *SS-Stubaf.* Siegfried Müller, the only unit that had remained inactive until then, was ordered to eliminate this dangerous salient enemy together with *SS-Pz.Gr.Rgt.26*; the German pioneers were considered elite infantry, specialized in assault operations and consequently there was a lot of confidence in their action. Under the cover of darkness, the pioneer assault teams were stationed south of Norrey, behind *3.Kp.* and *2.Kp./26*. On the right was *2.Kp./SS-Pz.Pi.Btl.12*, led by *SS-Ostuf.* Paul Kuret, in the center was *1.Kp.* of *Oberleutnant* Otto Toll and on the left, the *3.Kp.* of *SS-Hstuf.* Gerhard Tiedtke. *SS-Ostuf.* Herbert Bischoff set up his *4.Kp.* mortar platoon alongside the *3.Kp.* The attack began while it was still dark, with SS units attempting to approach Canadian positions in silence, but were discovered nonetheless and a massive barrage of Allied mortars and artillery was immediately unleashed. The *1.Kp.* under Toll, managed in spite of everything to reach the outskirts of the village, sheltering as best it could in the ravines in the area and from there, the SS pioneers began to respond to enemy fire. As soon as Allied resistance seemed to wane, *Oberleutnant* Toll ordered an attack against the enemy positions from the front, but the Canadians responded with machine guns, killing many victims among the SS pioneers, including Toll himself, who was seriously injured and then died shortly after due to the serious injuries he had received. What was left of the company fell back to its starting positions, bringing all the wounded back to the area southwest of Norrey.

June 9, 1944, Panthers of *3.Pz.Kp.* cross the Rue de la Villeneuve, in Rots. In the foreground is a scout of the *15.(Aufkl).Kp/SS-Pz.Gr.Rgt.25* in his *Schwimmwagen*. (US NARA)

A *Hitlerjugend Panther* in Normandy.

The command of the company then passed to SS-*Ustuf.* Bruno Asmus. The attack by the other pioneer companies was also unsuccessful, again due to the massive barrage by the Canadians. In the end, the losses for the battalion were significant: three officers, three non-commissioned officers and 22 dead soldiers, not counting the wounded and the missing.

Panther '318' of SS-Uscha. **Horst Maertz (US NARA).**

Defensive combat of SS-Pz.Gr.Rgt.25

After its attack, *SS-Pz.Gr.Rgt.25* had gone on the defensive, while the Canadian units had already crossed the Caen-Bayeux road, west of the Mue ridge. With the other units of the division engaged in the attack to the north, the Allies resumed their attacks in the sector occupied by Meyer's men, with the aim of conquering the Caen area. Thanks to fire support by *III./SS-Pz.Art.Rgt.12* and initially of *II./SS-Pz.Abt.12*, *SS-Pz.Gr.Rgt.25* prepared to parry the blow . The *Panzer Abteilung* was engaged as a mobile anti-tank force waiting for *SS-Pz.Jg.Abt.12* to receive its tank destroyers. On 8 June, British artillery began to hit the regiment's positions and during the same day, there were attacks of infantry units supported by tanks against the positions of the *I.* and *II.Bataillon*: at least two Allied tanks were destroyed by fire of the anti-tank guns. On 9 June, the Royal Ulsters attacked again, moving from Anisy in the afternoon, with the aim of seizing Cambes: to support it was the artillery of the 3rd Division and that of a cruiser offshore. However, when the battalion got to within about a kilometer from its target, it fell under the concentrated fire of German artillery, mortars and machine guns, sustaining serious losses. During the fighting on 9

SS-Ustuf. **Heinz-Hugo John.**

June, the commander of *7.Pz.Kp.*, *SS-Ostuf*, Heinz-Hugo John fell in combat; born in Erfurt in 1904, at the beginning of the war he served in the army, obtaining both classes of the Iron Cross. He was transferred to *Hitlerjugend* in 1943, when his training began. He had participated in the attack on 7 June, as commander of the *I. Zug* of *7.Pz.Kp*. After *SS-Hstuf.* Heinrich Bräcker was wounded, he had assumed command of the company.

A German *Panther* on Normandy front, June 1944.

Hitlerjugend Panther destroyed in the Norrey area, June 1944.

In the unit's daily report, his loss was reported as follows: "... *SS-Ostuf. Heinz John was killed in action on June 9, 1944 at around 8:00 pm, near La Folie, as commander of company of 7./SS-Pz.Rgt.12. The mission of the company was to protect the positions from attacks by enemy tanks and infantry. The area where the company had gathered was suddenly under mortar fire. Ostuf. John received the radio order to go to the Abteilung command post to receive further orders. Just as the Ostuf. was about to jump out of the Panzer, a direct shot hit the radio operator's hatch. A large piece of shrapnel hit Ostuf. John in the spine, killing him instantly. The radio operator, SS-Sturmmann Mende and the loader, SS-Schütze Noa were also killed. The driver and gunner managed to evacuate the vehicle in time and reach the command post of the Abteilung ...* ".

Bibliography
Massimiliano Afiero, "12th SS Panzer Division Hitlerjugend: From Formation to the Battle of Caen", Casemate Pub & Book Dist Llc

The French Volunteer Legion on the Eastern Front, 1943-1944

by Antonio Guerra

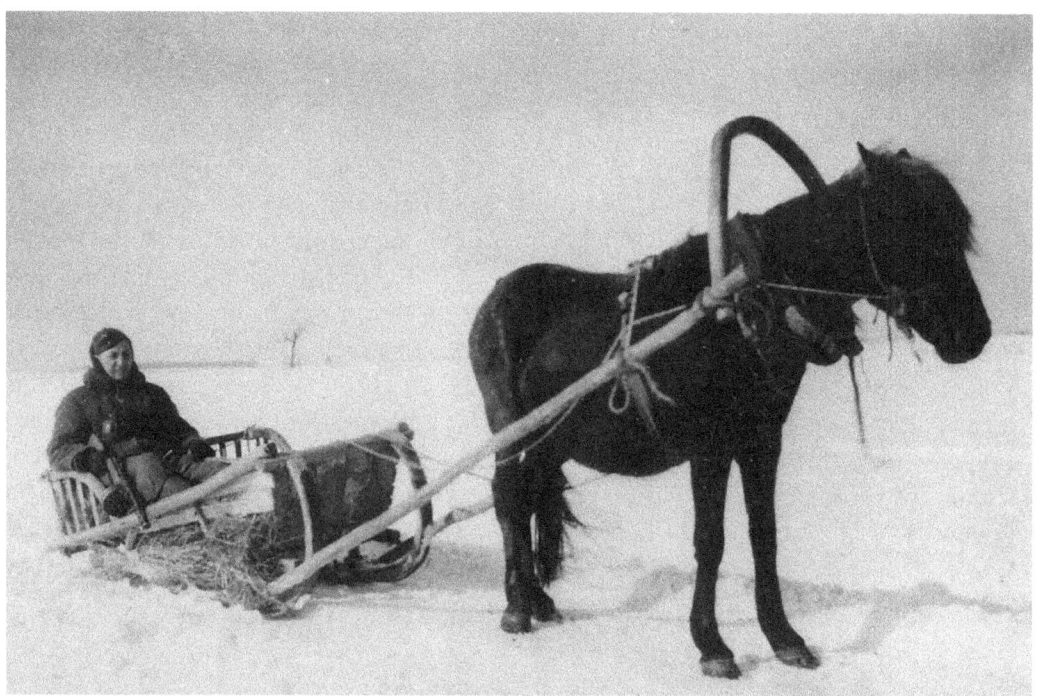

A 3rd Battalion volunteer on a sled during winter operations in early 1943 (*Chris Chatelet*).

3rd Battalion French volunteers during an attack, 1943.

Mamajevka Forest

At the beginning of 1943, the French III battalion, temporarily under the orders of Captain Jacques Madec, was engaged in mopping up and patrolling actions in the Mamajevka forest. At the beginning of February, the battalion was moved along the Desna to participate in a major German counteroffensive in the Kursk sector against Soviet forces. Between Orel and Kursk there had been a Soviet penetration into a sector where German forces were almost absent. The III battalion of the LVF then passed to the *2.Panzer-Armee* to plug the leak. It was necessary to stop the Soviet assaults along the Desna at all costs: the headquarters of the French battalion was installed in Ostraya Louka together with the

11.*Kompanie*; the 9.*Kompanie* took up positions on the left in the village of Gvinelo alongside a Hungarian unit, while the 10.*Kompanie* took up a position in Dolsk along with an Ostbataillon of Kyrgyz volunteers. The Soviet units on the other bank of the Desna had solidly fortified themselves but showed no sign of wanting to attack. The French legionaries were then ordered to carry out reconnaissance to detect the positions and size of the enemy forces. French scout patrols clashed with Soviet patrols, sent by the enemy for the same purpose. In the end, when the German armored formations of the 2nd Panzer Army intervened en masse, they managed to close the Soviet forces beyond the Desna into a pocket: the infantry units then intervened, including the French legionnaires, to annihilate the last pockets of enemy resistance.

A French volunteers in a Russian village, 1943.

Reunion of the two Battalions

From the beginning of June 1943, the two LVF battalions returned to operate in the same sector, controlling the area between Borissov and Tolocin to the north, the Tolocin-Krugloje-Moghilev road to the east, the course of the Beresina up to Murovo to the west. The 1st Battalion settled in the western part of the sector, the III in the eastern part: Major Eugène Panné, commander of the 3rd Battalion from the end of January 1943, established his command post in Krugloje. Having to face the continuously moving partisan forces, the Legion divided its forces between the various villages, establishing, as always, continuous liaison and patrolling actions. In this period, the two battalions of the LVF were operationally subordinate to the *286.Sicherungs-Division*. The *10.Kompanie* of the III battalion, under the orders of Captain Raymond Dewitte, was particularly involved in very tough clashes. On 9 June, the German headquarters of the *286.Sicherungs-Division* requested Captain Dewitte

A French volunteer on the Eastern front, 1943.

for a

Legionaries of the *10.Kompanie* of the LVF cross a bridge during an anti-partisan operation, June 1943.

French legionaries during an attack in a russian village.

III/LVF legionaries interrogate a Russian civilian, 1943.

security team for the technicians in charge of repairing the telephone line cut by the partisans, on the Moghilev-Bobruisk road beyond the Vaprinka river. A team of 16 legionaries was organized, loaded onto a single truck without any forward security element. The road passed through the woods and for the partisans it was almost a joke to set up an ambush: stationed at the edge of the woods, as soon as the partisans spotted the truck with the legionaries, opened fire with all their weapons: only the driver, a Russian auxiliary, managed to escape the carnage and raise the alarm. When the rescue patrols arrived on site, there was no trace of the partisans. Around the lorry, set on fire and looted, were sixteen naked and horribly mutilated corpses. Those who did not die immediately were ferociously massacred. From that moment, throughout the area along the Berezina, the partisans redoubled their efforts to prevent the establishment of surveillance posts by the French legionaries. In that same period, within the Legion, a special section was created, called the "*Chasse*" (the Hunt), an independent unit not linked to any company to be used as an emergency formation and to rescue other units in danger. Its main function, however, was to carry out coups and disruptive actions in villages occupied by the enemy. In practice the French wanted to use the same tactics as the partisans in controlling the territory,

The Axis Forces

Lieutenant Jacques Seveau.

A French legionnaire, armed with an MP-40 machine gun, during an attack on a village.

implementing the "*hit and run*" technique. The "*Chasse*" was placed under the orders of second lieutenant Jacques Seveau.

Operations in the summer of 1943

On July 5, 1943, the Germans launched Operation *Zitadelle*, to attempt to eliminate Soviet forces in the Kursk salient. Soviet partisan forces were mobilized to carry out disruptive actions in the German rear. The French Legion therefore had to intensify its raids to safeguard the lines of communication. On July 18, elements of the Dewitte company were attacked in the village of Kolbovo: for twelve hours the French tenaciously resisted the continuous assaults of the partisans, forcing them to retreat. On the French side, five casualties were recorded. On 1 August, the partisans attacked the village of Dubovoje in force, but were promptly repelled by the French who suffered on the occasion of the loss of around twenty men, including killed and wounded. On the night between 7 and 8 August, the *11.Kompanie* of the III battalion was attacked near the Orechovka surveillance post; furious fighting followed, which saw the French first defend themselves brilliantly and then counterattack the Soviets, who were forced to retreat. On 11 August, a column of wagons with supplies and materials was in transit on the road between Sokolovici and Novopolje: following were about a hundred men from the 3rd Battalion, including some elements returning from leave and half of the effectives of the 9.Kompanie at Dubovoje. The column was under the orders of Captain Ernest Estel, who had recently arrived on the Eastern Front and was therefore not yet accustomed to the war of ambushes and surprise attacks. At a certain point, about halfway along the road, some legionaries noticed the presence of mines. The bumps in the ground along the road were proof of this. The column stopped and a skeptical legionnaire jumped onto one of these bulges to demonstrate that there was

French volunteers during a break in the fighting.

III/LVF legionaries in a Russian village, summer 1943.

nothing to fear. The moment he set his feet on the prominent spot, a strong explosion threw him into the air, 'mangling' his body. The detonation was also the signal for the start of the attack by the partisans, who began hitting the French column from the edges of the road with mortars and machine gun fire. Captain Estel was one of the first to fall, mowed down by an enemy burst. The other legionaries tried to take cover as best they could, but the wood of the wagons did not offer valid protection against enemy bullets. Some legionaries managed to reach some isbas a few meters from the track. Lieutenant Bérard led his men in a desperate bayonet charge, but they were all killed. The few remaining wounded were massacred by the Soviets without any mercy. This terrible ambush by the partisans was the most costly in human lives for the III Battalion in all of 1943.

The Legion is reborn

The Legion's very high losses were offset by the arrival of a new second battalion formed with volunteers who had just finished training. The II Battalion, officially formed in November 1943, was placed under the command of Major Jean Tramu. In this way the Legion could be brought back to the strength of a real infantry regiment: the three battalions were reorganized and placed under the orders of Colonel Edgar Puaud[1].

Colonel Edgar Puaud in French uniform (Chatelet).

An antitank gun of the LVF in combat, 1943.

Order of battle September-November 1943

Commander: Colonel Edgar Puaud

Staff Company: Captain Guiraud

1st battalion
Commander: Captain Jean Bassompierre, Captain Jean Bridoux (from Nov. 1943)
1.Kompanie: Captain Jean Boudet-Gheusi
2.Kompanie: Lieutenant Alfred Falcy
3.Kompanie: Lieutenant Noël Piqué

2nd battalion
Commander: Major Jean Tramu
5.Kompanie: Lieutenant Guillaume Veyrieras
6.Kompanie: Captain Jean-Marie Pruvost
7.Kompanie: Lieutenant Roger Audibert

3rd battalion
Commander: Major Eugène Panné
9.Kompanie: Lieutenant Raymond Gaillard, Lieutenant Bernard Boillot (from November 1943)
10.Kompanie: Lieutenant Bernard Boillot, Lieutenant Maurice Berret (from November 1943)
11.Kompanie: Lieutenant Jean Neveux

On the Berezina front

At the beginning of October 1943, the Germans launched a series of attacks in the area east of the Berezina, against the partisan forces: the units of the III Battalion of the LVF also participated in the operations, which were engaged in the maneuver to encircle the enemy forces . During the operation, hundreds of rebels were captured and numerous of their camps were destroyed. At the beginning of November, the 1st Battalion, under the orders of the new commander, Captain Bridoux, son of the war minister of the Vichy government, participated in the capture of the village of Kononovici, which had fallen into the hands of the partisans. At the beginning of December, French patrols managed to identify the area where the partisan forces met and passed to transport their materials from one sector to another. Numerous enemy columns had been spotted passing through the village of Solovitchy several times. This time it was the French legionaries who organized an ambush on the partisans: a combat group was then formed, including two platoons of the 10.Kompanie and

Seveau's 'Chasse'. With a temperature of minus twenty degrees, the legionaries approached the village at night, taking up positions along the edges of the road that crossed it. The wait didn't last long: a column of enemy carts was spotted immediately afterwards. As soon as they were within range, the French machine guns and mortars opened fire and grenades were thrown: the carts blew up, hit by mortar fire, while the partisans fell one by one, mowed down by machine gun fire.

A French patrol marching on snowy terrain, 1943.

French legionnaires cross a river during a sweep to eliminate partisan forces, 1944.

However, from the number of carts destroyed, Seveau realized that what they had destroyed was only the vanguard: the bulk of the forces had yet to pass. It was necessary to clear the road of corpses and destroyed carts to prepare for the new ambush. After a few hours, another column was sighted, this time larger. Seveau ordered, "*Shoot only at my command.*" The entire column had to be within range to avoid possible escapes or counterattacks by the enemy. As soon as the column entered the road that crossed the village, the French waited for the first carts to pass, then

From the left, Jacques Doriot and lieutnant Seveau.

A German MG-34 supports a partisan attack.

at Seveau's order the target shooting began. Again explosions, carts were overturned, men falling under the crossfire of the French legionaries. Some partisans managed to take shelter behind their carts or behind some ridges on the ground and began to respond to fire. A group of Soviets launched an assault on the French positions in a desperate attempt to escape death, but they were all massacred. At the end of the fighting, Seveau and his men left the area. The booty had already been high and the ammunition was starting to run low; furthermore, the wounded, in need of medical care, had to be brought back. The Soviet wounded were left on the spot and Seveau, turning to one of them, who looked to be very proud, said: "*you can tell your comrades that the French don't kill enemy wounded*". For the action at Solovitchy, Seveau was promoted to lieutenant and decorated with the Iron Cross First Class.

The Somry Forest

On January 27, 1944, the French legionaries took part in a major offensive in the Somry forest, where according to the German command around six thousand partisans were hidden; thanks to an airfield built southwest of Saoserje, the partisans were able to receive weapons and supplies from the Red Army. Furthermore, among them there were also many soldiers of the Soviet regular army, who had parachuted into the area in the previous weeks. For the first time in its history, the Legion was employed in the same full operation, with all three of its battalions.

French legionaries engaged in combat, 1944.

Captain Bridoux in French uniform.

The Germans committed to the operation several Wehrmacht battalions and some Ostbataillonen, the battalions made up of anti-communist Russian volunteers.

On January 30, elements of the III Battalion attacked the village of Kosel, defended by partisans. The French legionaries decided to capture it with the bayonet, without waiting for fire support from the mortars. A French company attacked frontally, supported on the left by other elements of the 3rd Battalion and on the right by units of the 1st Battalion. As soon as they arrived at the first isbas of the village, the legionaries came under enemy fire and were forced to take cover in the snow. At that point the mortars intervened, while from the rear the Germans began to hit the Soviet positions with the 150 mm cannons placed in battery at Scepelevici. The isbas of the village caught fire, forcing the partisans to come out into the open: the well-positioned French machine guns exterminated the fugitives.

From the last isbas not yet in flames, a desperate counter-offensive began which crashed against the wall of fire of the French legionaries.

The sweep operations in the Somry forest and its surroundings continued for about fifteen days; after Kosel, the villages of Saoserje and Gorenka were conquered. In the end, a thousand prisoners were captured, although the bulk of the partisan forces managed to avoid capture and annihilation.

French legionaries during an attack, 1944.

French volunteer armed with an MG-34.

Operation Morocco

Taking advantage of the temporary retreat of the bulk of the partisan forces towards the east, the Germans immediately set up a new operation, agreed and planned with the collaboration of Commander Puaud, which was given the code name "*Operation Morocco*" in his honor. The idea was to go around the enemy positions in the retreat phase and trap them in a pocket, annihilating them. However, it was necessary to beat the enemy to the punch before he could reorganize his forces. On February 15, 1944, LVF units were loaded onto trucks and moved along the Bobruisk-Moghilev road. At the village of Cecerici, the French units carried out a 90° conversion towards the southeast, finding themselves right behind the enemy forces. On February 16, the legionaries began to march west, clashing with numerous enemy patrols and attacking Soviet camps; caught by surprise and caught between two fires, the partisans always got the worst of it, surrendering or ending up destroyed by the battle-hardened French, who instead suffered very few losses. Once again, however, success was not total: the bulk of the enemy forces managed to escape the enveloping maneuver. The OKW bulletin expressed itself positively despite everything, reporting that during the Morocco operation 41 partisan camps and 1,000 pillboxes had been destroyed, around 1,200 partisans had been killed and around 1,400 captured. On 18 February 1944, Major Panné fell in combat. Captain Berret took over command of the III Battalion. At the end of the operation, the 1st Battalion set off northwards to return to its sector of occupation east of the Beresina. On February 26, the battalion's units fell into an ambush in Devoscizi: covered by dense brush, the partisans attacked the moving French column. This time, however, the reaction of the legionaries was prompt: Captain Bridoux immediately had the men retreat along the edges of the forest.

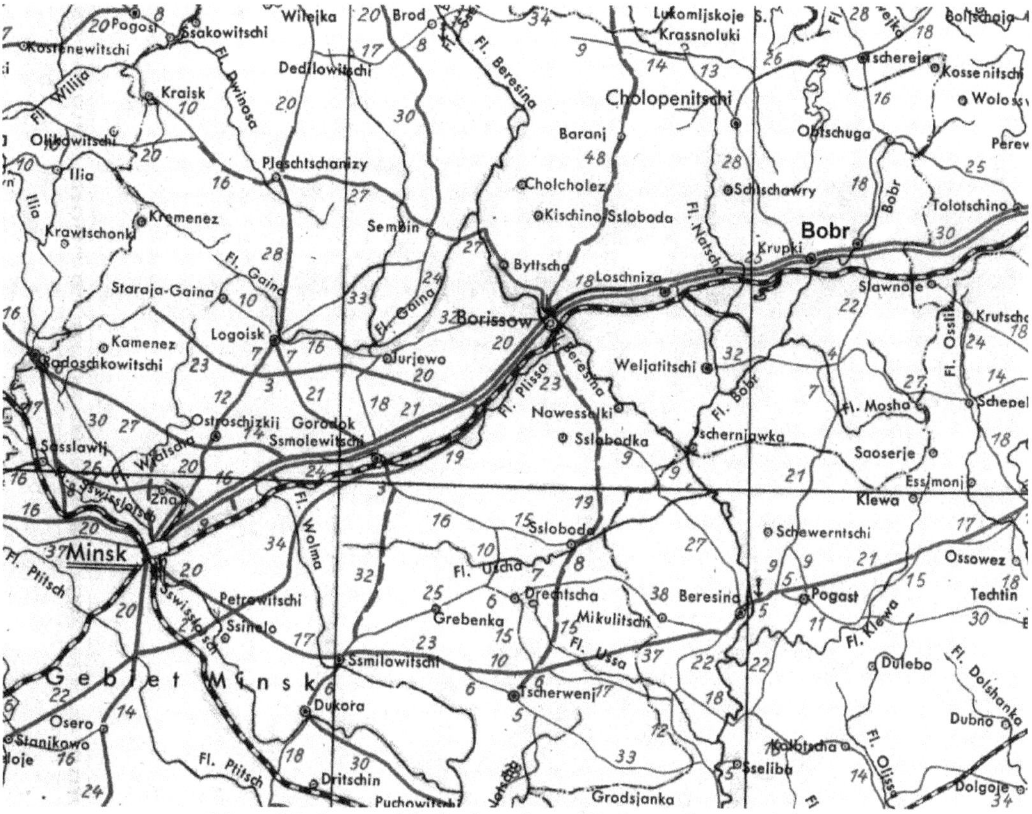

Map of Belarus with the location of Bobr on the top right.

German soldiers retreating on the Army Group Mitte front.

After putting the 80mm mortars and 37mm anti-tank guns into operation, the French began to hit the enemy positions with a powerful barrage. The partisans, given the violent response of the French, although outnumbered, preferred to retreat after three hours of intense fighting. Captain Bridoux was promoted to the rank of major for the valor demonstrated in combat. In April 1944, Commander Puaud traveled to France to participate in a recruitment drive for the LVF. Monsignor de Lupè and Jacques Doriot were also with him. On April 21, at the Vélodrome d'Hiver in Paris, Puaud addressed the audience hoping for mass participation of French youth in the fight against Bolshevism; the LVF could represent the rebirth of a new French army.

Monsignor de Lupè at the Vélodrome d'Hiver in Paris for the recruitment of new volunteers.

French legionnaires during a break in the fighting.

Commander Puaud returned to Russia in mid-May, bringing with him the forces of a company, the *13.Kompanie*, under the orders of Captain Émile Auffray, with which the formation of the IV Battalion of the LVF was started. Many Russian anti-communist volunteers had also been enrolled in the company.

The Marty Column

On 11 June 1944, a column was sent to patrol between Novo Polessy and Krutchka, an area where concentrations and movements of partisan forces had been reported. The column under the command of Captain Marty included two platoons of the *3.Kompanie* of the 1st Battalion under the command of Lieutenant Yves Rigeade and a platoon of cavalry under the command of Marshal Major Gabin, for a total of approximately 130 men. In the Marty column there was also Major Bridoux who had to return to his command post in Sokolovici. To cover the movement of the column, Puaud sent a detachment of the regimental company, about 60 men, under the command of Captain Henri Guiraud, with the task of moving north of Krutchka before Marty arrived with him. After a quiet start, the French scouts noticed suspicious movements in the direction of Krutchka; Captain Marty made his men change direction, abandoning the main road and making them march along the edges of the woods. Having arrived at the meeting point with Captain Guiraud's column near Krutchka, instead of finding their comrades they found themselves under enemy fire while crossing a stream: *"Take the wagons into the woods under cover"* shouted Captain Marty; the Soviet fire was concentrated at the point of the ford of the watercourse, an obligatory passage for the legionnaires. The partisans fired machine guns and mortars.

Two **French legionnaires engaged in combat on the Eastern front.**

German soldiers on a defensive position.

The French managed to place their machine guns and began to return enemy fire. Many fell, and only a few managed to find shelter immediately; Major Bridoux, considering the superiority of the enemy forces and finding himself facing not only partisans but also paratroopers of the Red Army, ordered the men to fall back. The disengagement was carried out in small groups through the bush, while the others had to continue shooting. After the barrage, the

Soviet infantry assaulting German positions.

Soviets attacked en masse; the French defended themselves by attacking with the bayonet. *"Long live the Legion"* shouted Lieutenant Rigeade, launching his men into the attack. The shouts and impetuosity of the French so frightened the Soviets that they were forced to retreat rather than engage in hand-to-hand combat with furious beasts. Taking advantage of the temporary enemy withdrawal, Bridoux and other legionaries managed to reach Novo Plessy, giving the alarm via radio to the regiment's command. Puaud, warned the German divisional command in Krupka requesting the immediate dispatch of armored vehicles. Meanwhile, the fate of the Guiraud detachment had been discovered: at 8:00 in the morning it had fallen into an enemy ambush and was completely annihilated. When Lieutenant Rigeade and Major Marshal Gabin arrived at the site of the ambush they found only a pile of corpses at the bottom of an embankment. At 1.00 pm, reinforcements finally arrived from Krupka, two trucks equipped with twin machine guns as well as a company of German infantry,

German defensive positions subjected to attacks and heavy bombardments by Soviet artillery, June 1944.

which forced the Soviet units to retreat definitively. In the Krutchka woods, the French Volunteer Legion had lost more than one hundred men, both fallen and missing.

The clashes on the Bobr front

On June 22, 1944, the fourth anniversary of the start of Operation Barbarossa (Stalin chose the date specifically), the general Soviet offensive against Army Group Center was launched. Three Soviet fronts, the 1st, 2nd and 3rd Belorussian Fronts, jointly attacked the positions of Army Group Mitte. At the same time, the partisan forces behind the German lines intensified their activity in an attempt to cut off all communication routes: thousands of explosions blew up the railway lines and main bridges from the Dnieper to the area west of Minsk. In the German rear there were only confusion and retreats.

German infantry units fall back to the Minsk front, summer 1944.

A group of French legionnaires on the Eastern front.

The units of the French Legion crossed the Bobr River, a tributary of the Berezina, following the retreat of the German forces; then they had to go back. Commander Puaud had received the order to bring his legionaries back to the front line: the LVF had to defend the Bobr sector, to cover the retreat of the other German units. The Todt organization had already built special trenches for the French along the Minsk-Moscow highway, through which the Soviet tanks would certainly have passed. A *Kampfgruppe* was formed under the orders of Major Bridoux, including the three companies of the 1st Battalion, two companies of the III, the *13.Kompanie* of the IV and the anti-tank unit: 600 men in all. With them also the German liaison officer of the Legion, *Oberst* von Spee. Arriving at the village of Bobr, the French took up positions in front of the highway bridge over the river of the same name: Lieutenant Yves Rigeade's

3.Kompanie placed its machine guns and mortars in the cemetery, among the graves. The *2.Kompanie* settled in the trenches that reached the highway with the heavy mortar group. The anti-tank guns landed to the right of the road to Bobr. The French defensive position was excellent, being elevated above the enemy's area of advance. *Oberst* von Spee also managed to have four Tiger tanks[2] arrive as reinforcements: two took up positions at the edge of the woods, camouflaging themselves appropriately, while the other two positioned themselves on the sides of the highway.

A *Tiger* tank of the *s.Pz.Abt.505* on the Eastern front, summer 1944.

Hauptmann von Beschwitz.

Their 88mm guns would have lent a hand to the scarce 37mm anti-tank guns supplied to the French units. On June 24, the Soviets attacked the positions held by the French: the tanks began to arrive first and stopped halfway, awaiting the arrival of the supporting infantry. Puaud arrived among his men in the front line shouting: "*we must hold on as long as possible*". The four Tiger tanks with their precise and powerful fire destroyed the Soviet tanks one by one. The French mortars and machine guns instead dealt with the Soviet infantry, who were immediately put to flight. During the night, elements of an SS Police regiment arrived to support the French, also bringing with them some 75mm anti-tank guns. At dawn on 26 June, the Soviet artillery began to hit the Franco-German positions: at the aid station of Doctor Pierre Métais, medical officer within the 1st Battalion, the first wounded began to arrive with their bodies torn apart by the explosions. Losses increased significantly when the Soviets also began to use Katyusha rocket launchers. The Soviet infantry attacked immediately after the village of Bobr: the first to be attacked were the legionaries of the Rigeade company, stationed in the cemetery. Led by their commander, the French managed to repel the Soviets after furious fighting, during which Rigeade himself was seriously wounded in the head; second lieutenant Michel de Genouillac took his place.

German defensive position along the Berezina river, subjected to Soviet artillery fire, 1944.

A Tiger of *s.Pz.Abt.505* engaged in combat, summer 1944.

After a period of relative calm, the Soviets returned to the attack; this time with an entire armored formation of around fifty tanks; Major Bridoux gave the alarm to the Tigers of *s.Pz.Abt.505*. The German tank commander reassured the Frenchman: *"Let the tanks pass, we'll take care of it, you think of the infantry."* The Tigers opened fire at a great distance, massacring *T-34s* and *Sherman* tanks. Many Soviet tanks were also destroyed thanks to the fire of 75mm anti-tank guns. The battlefield was filled with the carcasses of destroyed tanks, preventing enemy tanks from advancing and

A Soviet T-34 tank with infantry on board.

Tiger tanks in combat on the Eastern front, 1944.

Soviet Infantry during an attack, summer 1944.

continuing further. Six Soviet tanks managed to get close to the German positions: four were immediately destroyed by the Tigers, the other two by the French 37mm anti-tank guns. The French were ordered to continue resisting. At 11pm on June 26, the Soviets launched a new attack in force. The Bobr cemetery fell into their hands, after the remnants of the French company had been massacred to the last one. The Tiger tanks stopped the advance of the enemy tanks, giving the French the opportunity to counterattack; the legionnaires attacked the cemetery, dislodging the Soviets after furious hand-to-hand fighting.

At dawn on June 27, the Soviets returned to the assault: a mass of armored vehicles swept across the plain followed by an equally large mass of infantry. The Tiger fire continued to wreak havoc on Soviet tanks while the infantry fell under fire from French heavy weapons. Three Soviet tanks managed to reach the cemetery, but the anti-tank guns under the orders of Lieutenant Noël Piqué, hidden right there, destroyed two of them. At the moment of hitting the third tank, Piqué himself fell under enemy fire. By 8:00 in the morning the Soviets had managed to establish themselves north of the cemetery and along the railway. Just as the Soviets were about to launch a new assault, Puaud arrived at 9:00 with the order to retreat. In Bobr, despite the violence of the fighting, the French Legion had recorded the loss of 41 dead and 24 wounded. 57 Soviet tanks had been destroyed, and

French legionaries with a Russian civilian, 1944.

the plain in front of Bobr was strewn with hundreds of Soviet corpses. The sacrifice of the French at Bobr in delaying the enemy advance had allowed the evacuation of thousands of wounded from the hospitals of Borissov and Minsk and the German units to be able to withdraw in an orderly manner. On 28 June 1944, an official statement from the Red Army reported: "*On the Bobr River, armored units belonging to the 2nd Byelorussian Front were stopped by the fierce resistance of two French divisions*"(3).

On the Minsk front

Once the Vitebsk-Orscha-Moghilev-Bobruisk defensive line fell, Hitler ordered his generals to establish a new defensive line along the course of the Berezina. The French legion together with other German units were thus busy establishing a bridgehead on the eastern bank of the Berezina in front of Borissov. On the afternoon of June 28, Lieutenant Jean Fatin with his *1.Kompanie* together with the survivors of the III Battalion settled along the highway east of Borissov. During the night, on the same day, Major Bridoux managed to recover the two companies of the 1st Battalion south of Laonitza. The legionaries were short of equipment and ammunition. The II Battalion under the orders of Major Tramu, from Moghilev, semi-surrounded by Soviet forces, headed towards Belynici, where it covered the retreat to the *Panzergrenadier-Division Feldherrnhalle*, fighting simultaneously against the Red Army and the partisan forces. Meanwhile, on the Borissov bridgehead, Fatin's company was already fighting against the Soviet avant-garde; Without the support of tanks and heavy weapons, it seemed impossible for the French to repel the assault of the Soviet armored formations.

Major Jean Bridoux.

A 37mm anti-tank gun engaged in combat.

The few 37mm anti-tank guns barely made a dent in the armor of enemy tanks unless they were at a distance of less than fifty meters, i.e. a suicide distance for the gun's crew. The defensive fighting lasted until June 30th, then Puaud was forced to order a retreat, which he personally led. Taking advantage of a moment of relative calm in the sector and covered by the supporting fire of some German units, the French legionaries retreated towards the west. After fighting in Belynici, the men of the II Battalion also crossed the Berezina to join the remnants of the Legion: the regrouping of the various French units took place a few kilometers east of Minsk. On July 1, the Soviets began to tighten their grip around the city, attacking from the northeast and southeast. Puaud received orders to commit his men to the defense of Misk: Major Bridoux with the remnants of the 1st Battalion were sent to defend an ammunition depot south of the city. On July 3, the Soviets entered Minsk and the French had no choice but to retreat further west. However, more than half of the Legion's forces were left behind: fallen, wounded and missing. Starting from 9 July, all the survivors of the LVF were withdrawn from the front and sent towards Kaunas in Lithuania where they were regrouped and where they remained until 15 July. On July 18, they were transferred to the Greiffenberg camp in East Prussia. Here, they awaited their transfer to the *Waffen-SS*, to form a new French unit which was to accommodate all the French volunteers enlisted in the various German units.

Notes

[1] Edgar Puaud was born on 29 October 1889 in Orlèans. He was orphaned at an early age. Encouraged by his guardian, the young Puaud turned towards a military career, entering the military school of Saint-Maixent from where he graduated as a non-commissioned officer. In 1914, at the outbreak of the First World War, he was already a second lieutenant in a unit of Alpine troops. Shortly afterwards he joined an infantry regiment fighting on the front lines against the Germans. In November 1918 he reached the rank of captain. After leaving the army, Puaud joined the Foreign Legion in 1923. He served in Morocco, then in Syria and Indochina, where he was promoted to the rank of Major. After the French defeat in 1940, Puaud entered the Vichy army, as commander of the III Battalion of the 23rd Infantry Regiment located in Montauban. Promoted to lieutenant colonel he assumed command of the regiment until the summer of 1942, when he was transferred to Agen to direct the local office of the Foreign Legion. In July 1942, he enlisted in the Tricolor Legion; appointed colonel in December, he assumed the position of inspector general of the LVF, leaving for the Eastern front. In September 1943, appointed colonel of the *Wehrmacht*, he received command of the LVF.

[2] These were the Tigers of the *Schwere Panzer-Abteilung 505*, under the orders of *Hauptmann* Werner Freiherr von Beschwitz. The heavy armored battalion was engaged at the end of June 1944 in the Bobr sector, on the western bank of the river, fighting at Ossinowka, Krupki and destroying numerous Soviet tanks.

[3] R. Forbes, "*For Europe: The French volunteers of the Waffen-SS*", page 135.

Bibliography

Massimiliano Afiero, "*I volontari stranieri di Hitler*", Ritter edizioni
Christophe Leguérendais, "*Sotto le insegne del Terzo Reich*", L'Assalto Edizioni
Jean Mabire, Éric Lefebvre, "*Sur les pistes de la Russie Centrale. Les Français de la LVF 1943*", Grancher
Wolfgang Schneider, "*Tigers in Combat I*", Stackpole Books

The 11th Nordland division and the defense of the Baltic countries

by Massimiliano Afiero

Soviet offensives on the Baltic Front, Summer-Autumn 1944.

Sd.Kfz.222 of 2./SS.Pz.Aufkl.Abt.11 in Estonia, Summer 1944.

New soviet attacks

While fighting was under way at the Narva bridgehead, the Soviets made an encircling attack from the south, towards Latvia and Lithuania, with the aim of capturing Riga, the capital of Latvia and to cut the German defensive dispositions in the Baltic region in two.

After having crossed the Neva River south of Lake Peipus and the city of Pleskau, the Soviet forces headed north to take the German forces still stationed on the northern Estonian front from the rear.

The Germans were thus forced to abandon the positions that they had held since February 1944 in order to attempt to establish a new defensive line, oriented to the southeast, along the Pleskau-Jakobstadt railway line, with the city of Tartu (Dorpat in German) in the center.

The Soviets lost no time in attacking this new German line of resistance, shifting their offensive to the northeast, between Lake Peipus and the small Lake Virz (Vörtsjärv).

The SS-Pz.Aufkl.Abt.11 in action

SS-Stubaf. **Rudolf Saalbach.**

Heeresgruppe Nord was asked to transfer all available forces to the area of the breakthrough and *III.(germ.)SS-Pz.Korps* decided to send *SS-Panzer-Aufklärungs-Abteilung 11*, led by *SS-Stubaf.* Rudolf Saalbach. The *Nordland* recon group was moved by train to Dünaburg (Daugavpils). Because the Soviet advance was very rapid, the unit was moved further to the rear, to the northwest, to the Jakobstadt (Jekabpils), where it arrived on July 10, 1944. On July 14, it was decided to organize a combat group to restore contact between *Heeresgruppe Nord* and *Mitte*. The *Kampfgruppe* was placed under command of *General der Kavallerie* Philipp Kleffel and consisted of *61.Inf.Div., 225.Inf.Div.* and *SS-Pz.Aufkl.Abt.11*. The *Kampfgruppe* went on the attack and some of its elements were soon able to make contact with *Heeresgruppe Mitte* forces. But the area was too vast and this contact broke down almost immediately. *Panzergruppe Saalbach*, with its armored vehicles and half-tracks, proved to be an effective and extremely mobile force, engaged in the most threatened points of the front. The SS troops carried out reconnaissance, rapid counterattacks and were used to close gaps in the defensive front.

An *SS-Untersturmführer* of *SS-Pz.Aufkl.Abt.11* on board his *Sd.Kfz.250* armed with an MG-42.

Kampfgruppe Saalbach soon became a sort of phantom unit, whose armored cars appeared unexpectedly, bringing death or confusion among enemy positions, then to disappear again. Soon after, they were in action again in another sector of the front. Further south, Soviet forces were continuing to advance, especially in the Polozk area.

Other photo of the *SS-Untersturmführer* on board his *Sd.Kfz.250*.

Generalmajor Hyazinth Graf Strachwitz.

The Tiger tanks of *Schwere-Panzer-Abteilung 502* sought to halt the enemy advance, managing to destroy numerous Soviet tanks. Other enemy tanks were knocked out from above by the *Stukas* of *Major* Hans Rudel. Nevertheless, on July 24, Dünaburg was captured by Soviet forces.

A few days later, Soviet forces were able to reach the coast of the Gulf of Riga, not near the capital, but a little more to the west, at Tukums, where the most violent fighting on the Latvian front broke out. The last of the *Wehrmacht's* panzers were concentrated and thrown into a counterattack, led by *Generalmajor* Hyazinth Graf Strachwitz, but in the end only about a dozen tanks and 15 half-tracks were scraped together. Only after having received other reinforcements,

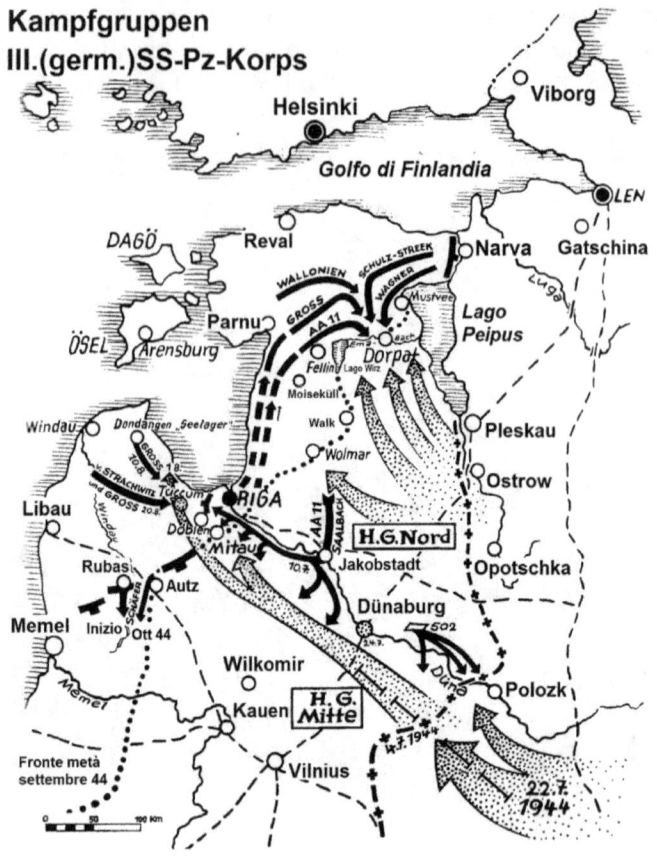

Movement of *SS Kampfgruppen* Summer-Autumn 1944.

Panther and German grenadiers on the Latvian front, 1944.

among them the *Panzer-Brigade-Gross*, *Generalmajor* Strachwitz was able to attack and retake Tukums on August 20, 1944.

Kampfgruppe Wagner

Stalled in the south, the Soviets resumed their attack further north, between Lake Peipus and Lake Virz, in the Dorpat (Tartu) peninsula. A defensive line was hastily formed to contain the Soviets who were advancing from Pleskau (Pskov), south of Lake Peipus. In the Tartu area the German headquarters decided to launch a counteroffensive to cover the retreat of German troops towards Latvia and to contain the Soviet assault made south of Lak Peipus. *SS-Ogruf.* Steiner was ordered to send troops to the south to block the Soviet advance and to that end a *Kampfgruppe* was formed under *SS-Brigdf.* Jürgen Wagner[1], the *Nederland* brigade commander, consisting of elements of the Dutch brigade (the rest of the brigade remained on the *Tannebergstellung* under *Oberst* Friedrich), *I./Waffen-Gr.Rgt.d.SS 45*, the *I.* and *II./Waffen-Gr.Rgt. 46*, a combat group of the *SS Wallonien* assault brigade, *Grenadier Regiment 23* of the *11.Inf.Div.,SS-Panzer-Aufklärungs-Abteilung 11* (already transferred to the area), a company of *SS-Pz.Jg.Abt.54*, the *II./SS-Art.Rgt.54*, several army artillery groups and rocket launcher batteries, and the last of the *Nordland's* assault guns. During the night between August 15 and 16, the units of the just formed *Kampfgruppe Wagner* were withdrawn from their positions on the *Tannenbergstellung* and from the rear areas of *III.(germ.)SS-Panzer-Korps*.

SS-Brigdf. **Wagner (left in photo) in a *'Nordland'* defensive position, personally awarding iron crosses to several soldiers, Summer 1944.**

An *SS-Rottenführer* of *SS-StuG.Abt.11*.

The combat group of the *SS Wallonien* assault brigade came directly from the Debica training camp, where the unit was being reorganized. Organized as a battalion with 452 men, commanded by *SS-Hstuf.* Georges Ruelle, it was later led by *SS-Stubaf.* Leon Degrelle[2]. Degrelle reached the Baltic front on 8 August to personally lead his Walloon volunteers in combat.

On August 16, *SS-Art.Rgt.54*, led by *SS-Hstuf.* Quintus de Veer, left from the Jöwhi railway station in Dorpat, where the other units of the *Kampfgruppe* also arrived. Based on orders from the high command, the defensive line of *Kampfgruppe Wagner* was to run from Lake Virz to southeast of Lake Peipus; the course of the River Embach (Ema) that connected the two lakes was to have constituted the natural combat line if the Soviets had been able to get close to the Tartu area.

From the left, *SS-Brigdf*. Wagner, *SS-Stubaf*. Léon Degrelle and *SS-Ostuf*. Karl Schäfer, Degrelle's German aide.

Members of an Estonian border regiment, Dorpat sector.

Aerial view of Dorpat crossed by the river Embach, 1944.

Organization of the defenses

At Tartu, *SS-Brigdf*. Wagner got together as many men as possible to reinforce his *Kampfgruppe*: among the civilian population, all men between the ages of 16 and 50 were recruited and armed with whatever was at hand; Estonian paramilitary forces were called up; the remnants of several German units were brought in, such as *Grenadier Regiment 23*, the *III./Werfer-Regiment 3* and *II./Artillerie-Regiment 58*, which had already been involved in the defense of the sector. The first units of the *Kampfgruppe* took up positions south of Tartu and several recon patrols were soon sent out throughout the area in order to intercept the Soviet advance elements in time. The two Walloon companies, numbering about three hundred men, were deployed along a line that ran from the road that led from Dorpat to Petseri, along Lake Peipus, to the road that ran from Dorpat to Valka towards the center of the town. *II./SS-Art.Rgt*. 54 emplaced its batteries on both sides of the city, but on August 20, were moved further forward by about twenty kilometers to the southeast in order to provide fire support to Estonian units and to *11.Infanterie-Division*. The Soviets assailed the thin defensive line with massive forces.

The Axis Forces

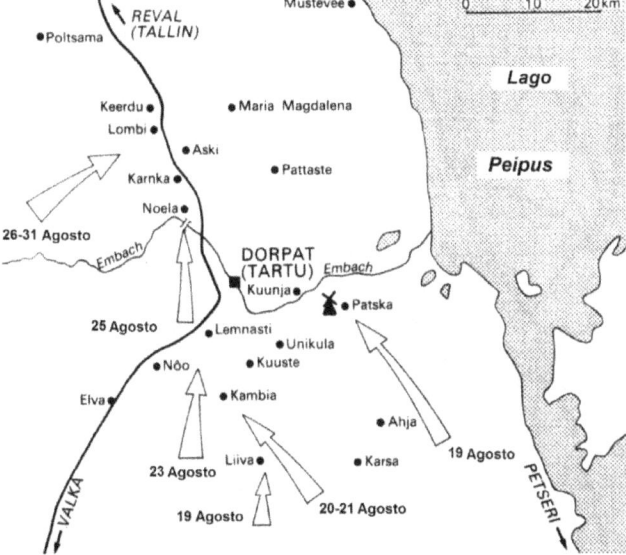

The defense of Dorpat, August 1944.

A German 105 mm howitzer engaged in battle.

A *Waffen-SS* 75 mm antitank gun in position, 1944.

The Estonians, badly armed and equipped, were easily overwhelmed. The 1st Company of *Füsilier-Bataillon 11* led by *Leutnant* Bucholz, on the left wing, bore the brunt of the enemy attack. The commander of *4./SS-Art.Rgt. 54, SS-Ustuf.* Günther Horstmann, quickly provided supporting fire, managing to throw the Soviets back. Soon after, the enemy returned to attack, employing greater forces. *SS-Ustuf.* Horstmann ordered his gunners to fire on the Soviets, once again stalling the Soviet attack. The Soviets answered with fire from their antitank guns, then resumed their attack. The German units were forced to withdraw to a new defensive line. *II./SS-Art.Rgt. 54* displaced to new firing positions at Meliste. On August 19, *SS-Brigdf.* Wagner ordered *SS-Stubaf.* Degrelle to halt the enemy penetration in the Kambi sector, providing several assault guns in support. Two Walloon companies were engaged in capturing the village of Patska, after which they had to del with successive Soviet counterattacks but were able to hold on to the position. When enemy pressure became very strong, the Walloon volunteers pulled back to positions further to the rear, continuing to repel the Soviet attacks. The Walloons did not abandon their position at Kambi until dawn on August 22 and then joined other units of the *Kampfgruppe*. Meanwhile, the Soviets had gotten past Unikula and had taken Kuunja,

SS-Ustuf. Léon Gillis on the Baltic front, 1944.

A 75 mm antitank gun in position on the Baltic front.

southeast of Dorpat, reaching the gates of Nôo, where another group of Walloon volunteers led by *SS-Ustuf.* Léon Gillis was in position with its three 75mm Pak guns and three 80mm mortars. When Nôo fell on August 23, Gillis' Walloon group withdrew to the northeast and this time the antitank guns were emplaced to defend the bridge over the River Embach at Voora. There the Soviets attacked with about a dozen Josef Stalin tanks; seeing those steel monsters, Gillis did not lose heart and ordered his men to prepare to fire. The antitank gun crews waited until the first tank got to within about thirty meters from their positions and then opened fire. The first tank was hit, going up in flames, then another tank was hit in the tracks and began to rotate on its own axis uncontrollably. Unexpected support came from a German artillery battery that was located not far from Valloni, whose fire added to the destruction of enemy tanks. Soviet infantry nevertheless attacked along with the surviving tanks. In short order the three Walloon antitank guns were destroyed and it was thanks only to the supporting fire of the German battery that the Walloons were able to pull back to new positions to the west of Dorpat and south of the crest of Em. On August 24, *Panzer-Brigade 101* and *SS-Panzer-Brigade Gross* moved against the positions at Elwa and Nôo, coming from Latvia. *SS-Pz.Aufkl.Abt.11*, led by *SS-Stubaf.* Rudolf Saalbach, with *Kampfgruppe Graf Strachwitz*, captured the village of Tamsa

The Axis Forces

Léon Degrelle on the march with his Walloons, 1944.

Half-tracks of *3.Kp./SS-Pz.Aufkl.Abt.11* on the march.

A short 75 mm gun mounted on an German *Sd.Kfz.251/9*. The white striped painted on the barrel indicate enemy tanks destroyed.

further to the north. Also on August 24, the Soviets reached the southern shore of Lake Virz, separating *Armee Abteilung Narwa* from *18.Armee*. The next Soviet objective was now represented by the port of Pärnu on the Gulf of Riga. In the meantime, *SS-Pz.Aufkl.Abt.11* was attached to *Kampfgruppe Wagner*, to be employed as a mobile quick reaction force.

The battle for Dorpat

The battle for Dorpat began on August 25; committed to its final defense were *I./Gren.Rgt.33*, the *I./StuG.Brigade 393* and Estonian units, which were able to hold their positions until the afternoon. By 18:00 the Soviets had taken Dorpat. *SS-Unterscharführer* Berthold Benke of *5.Kp./SS-Pz.Aufkl.Abt.11*, along with a handful of Germanic volunteers, continued to hold the Dorpat airfield with his *Sd.Kfz.251/9* half-track armed with a 75mm gun. The Soviets attacked with superior forces, but Behnke and the SS grenadiers drove them back. Once Dorpat had fallen, the Soviets crossed the river at Embach, establishing a bridgehead on the northern bank. *SS-Stubaf*. Degrelle had been ordered to set up a blocking position north of Dorpat along the Parna-Lombi-Keerdu line. The Walloon commander put all of the available men in the front line, including non-combatants and wounded soldiers still able to hold a weapon. After having managed to scrape up around sixty men, Degrelle led them to the outskirts of Dorpat where the presence of Soviet advance units had been reported. An initial attack was repulsed. Meanwhile, Degrelle had been able to find two artillery pieces that were hastily put in battery in the antitank role. Shortly thereafter he contacted Wagner via telephone to bring him up to date on the situation and to ask for reinforcements.

Léon Degrelle among his Walloon volunteers on the Estonian front, Summer 1944.

Walloon machine gunner in combat, 1944.

SS-Brigdf. Jürgen Wagner answered: '*...hold out at all costs. I'll send reinforcements as soon as I can*'. Degrelle repled: '*As long as I'm alive, the Soviets won't get through*'. After having managed to scrape together around another forty volunteers, Degrelle organized his hundred men into two combat groups, positioning them on both sides of the road that led to Dorpat and at the same time sent out recon patrols to determine the enemy's movements in a timely manner. The Soviets came back to attack in force, putting the resistance of the extreme defenders of Dorpat to the test, but just at the moment that they were about to overrun the enemy defenses, a squadron of Stuka dive-bombers came on the scene to repel them anew. Many enemy tanks were destroyed on the ground while Soviet infantry was forced to shelter in the nearby forest. Soon after, some Tiger tanks arrived to bolster the defenses.

For this exemplary conduct of defensive operations at Dorpat, on August 27, 1944, Léon Degrelle was awarded the Oak Leaves for his Knight's Cross.

Walloon volunteers in combat on the Estonian front, Summer 1944.

SS units in action

At the same time, the vehicles of *SS-Pz.Aufkl.Abt.11* continued to be busy in the hot spots in the front as a quick reaction force. Thus, on August 26, *SS-Standarten-Oberjunker* Walter Schwarck, a platoon leader in *5./SS-Pz.Aufkl.Abt.11*, was informed that the crews of two *Flak* guns and of two 105mm howitzers deployed in a defensive position had been surrounded in the village of Haage, running the risk of being overrun at any minute. His recon troopers jumped into their half-tracks armed with 75mm guns and quickly moved to the position freeing their comrades. The *Nordland* assault guns were also hard pressed in the Dorpat area; initially there were seven StuG from *SS-Pz.Abt.11* and six StuG from *SS-Pz.Jg.Abt.11* commanded by *SS-Hstuf*. Schulz-Streek.

An assault gun in ambush.

But soon, no one was left: *SS-Hstuf*. Hans-Karl Becker was the only officer left alive. Among those killed were *SS-Ustuf*. Heinz Stamm, commander of *2./SS-Pz.Abt.11* and *SS-Ustuf*. Ernst-

Richard Stübben, commander of *3./SS-Pz.Abt.11*. During the final days of August, the Walloon volunteers continued to hold their blocking positions along the Pärnu-Lombi-Keerdu line, repelling all of the Soviet attacks at great sacrifice.

SS-Stubaf. Degrelle award the Iron Cross to a wounded Walloon soldier, 1944.

SS grenadiers inspect a destroyed enemy tank.

Degrelle's men were cited three times in the order of the day of *III.(germ.)SS-Pz.Korps*. When the fighting was over, *SS-Ogruf.* Steiner awarded more than 200 Iron Crosses to the Walloon volunteers. Léon Gillis was awarded the Knight's Cross. A few days later, what was left of the Walloon battalion was transferred to Germany.

Operation Aster

On September 10, 1944, *SS-Obergruppenführer* Felix Steiner had to report to Hitler's headquarters at Rastenburg: Hitler communicated his intention of wishing to abandon Estonia but at the same time ordered *III.SS-Pz.Korps* to hold a bridgehead at Reval in order to allow evacuation of all German forces by sea. Returning to the Estonian front, Steiner met with *Generaloberst* Schörner, commander of Army Group North, to discuss the plans to evacuate Estonia, code named Operation *Aster*.

Führer headquarters, August 27, 1944. *SS-Stubaf.* **Léon Degrelle receiving the Oak Leaves for his Knight's Cross, directly from Adolf Hitler, in the presence of** *SS-Ogruf.* **Felix Steiner.**

SS grenadiers inspect a destroyed enemy tank.

On September 16, Soviet vanguards of the 3rd Baltic Front began to break into the Dorpat isthmus, establishing favorable positions for successive attacks between Dorpat and Lake Peipus. Two days later, Soviet forces reached Mustvee, near the northwest corner of Lake Peipus. The men of *SS-Pz.Aufkl.Abt.11* had to take action to cover the withdrawal of *III.(germ.)SS-Pz.*Korps from the *Tannenbergstellung*. The SS units began to withdraw to Latvia in the night between September 18 and 19, heading towards Pernau, on the northern coast of the Gulf of Riga, under the protection of *II.Armee-Korps*.

Waffen-SS grenadiers and destroyed *'Josef Stalin'* tanks, Summer 1944.

An antitank squad with a *Panzerschreck*, 1944.

Everything went according to plan: the *Norge* and *Danmark* regiments withdrew without problem and the next day the motor convoys reached Wesenberg where there was a large warehouse full of supplies. The SS soldiers took whatever they could before blowing it up. The Germanic volunteers were engaged in defensing the capital of Latvia, Reval and the port of Pernau. Thanks to the sacrifices of the European volunteers, German ships were able to evacuate more than 80,000 men from Reval in a few days, before the city fell in Soviet hands. The following day, Pernau also fell after having been defended for three days by *Kampfgruppe Bunse*, consisting of I./'de Ruyter' and other elements of the *Nederland*. Soon after, the *Nordland* recon battalion and *Kampfgruppe*

The Axis Forces

SS-Stubaf. Walter Plöw.

SS-Pz.Aufkl.Abt.11 half-tracks on the move.

Bunse withdrew to the south, with *Nordland* blocking the road to the Bay of Pärnu east of Moiseküll and the *Kampfgruppe* engaged in the Wolmar area. On September 24, *Kampfgruppe Petersen (II./'de Ruyter')* assumed positions along the River Lemmer south of Pärnu, blocking the coast road to the south. On the morning of September 25, the Dutch volunteers of *Kampfgruppe Petersen* were strung out along the coastal road on the border between Estonia and Latvia. Once Reval had fallen, other German units also retreated to the south along the coast. While units of *III.(germ.)SS-Pz.Korps* were withdrawing to the south, those of *XXVIII* and *L.Armee-Korps* continued to defend the Walk-Wolmar line, suffering heavy losses during bitter fighting. In particular, *21.Infanterie-Division* was overrun and reduced to a small *Kampfgruppe*. *SS-Flak-Abteilung 11* was attached to the *Kampfgruppe* of *21.Infanterie-Division*, being engaged in tough defensive fighting. When the fighting was over, the division commander, *Generalmajor* Heinrich Goetz, recommended the German Cross in Gold for *SS-Ostubaf.* Plöw, commander of *SS-Flak-Abteilung 11* and *SS-Ostuf.* Rolf Holzboog[3], commander of *4./SS-Flak-Abt.11*.

Clashes in the Baldone area

Stalled along the road to Riga, the soviets shifted their attacks more to the west, towards the city of Doblen (Dobele) about 60 kilometers southwest of Riga. The units of *III.SS-Pz.Korps* were to reach the Tukums area, the next fulcrum of defense on the Latvian front. Since September 22, the bulk of the *Nordland* units had entrenched in the great pine forests north of Kekava, southeast of Riga. The *Norge* regiment in particular had been grouped in the area between Dekmeri and Katlapji, while the divison's few armored vehicles had been concentrated in the Senbegi area. *I./SS-Art.Rgt.11* took up poisitons north of Tici. The *Danmark* regiment was subordinated to *14.Panzer-Division*, commanded by *Generalmajor* Oskar Munzel, who had been ordered to eject the Soviets from the city of Baldone, on the

River Kekava. The *Danmark* commander, *SS-Ostubaf.* Krügel, moved his command post to the village of Celmini, from where he could better follow the development of operations.

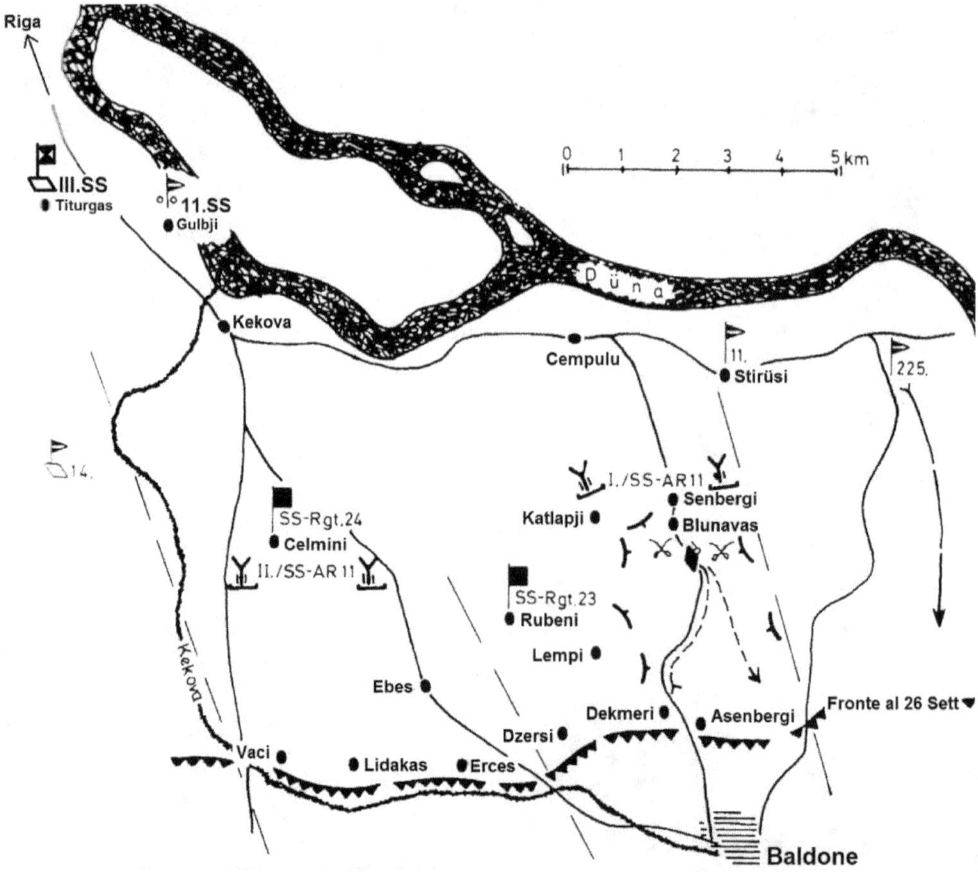

Combat in the area north of Baldone, September 23-26, 1944.

Waffen-SS defensive position on the Latvian front, 1944.

The attack was made the next day, employing the *II./24* under *SS-Hstuf.* Ternedde and the *III./24* under *SS-Hstuf.* Bergfeld[(4)]. The Soviets were initially forced back, thanks in part to supporting fire by German artillery and attacks by dive bombers which eliminated most of the enemy firing positions. Soon after, Likidas fell into SS hands. However, when those same units approached the Kekava river, they came under massive barrage fire from the Soviets, who had set up numerous antitank positions and many machine gun nests. The grenadiers of 6. and 11./*Danmark* were forced to take shelter in the woods. The arrival of tanks and assault guns from *14.Panzer-Division* served little, because of the difficult terrain the vehicles could not maneuver properly. The Soviets counterattacked soon after with infantry and tanks.

German grenadiers and soviet tanks destroyed at close range, Summer 1944.

SS grenadier and a destroyed tank.

Hundreds and hundreds of Soviet infantrymen popped up from everywhere, forcing the Danish grenadiers to fall back. The groups that stayed behind to fight were soon surrounded and cut off from other friendly forces. The officers requested artillery support via radio and soon after the German guns began to hit enemy positions on the southern bank of the Kekava. The Soviets responded quickly with their own artillery, mortars and *Katyusha* rocket launchers. Losses began to mount horrifically for both sides. Around 13:30, the enemy counterattack was somehow stemmed. The order was then given to resume the attack, sending tanks from *14.Panzer-Division* forward, followed by the *Danmark* grenadiers. But once again, the momentum of the German units was stalled near the Kekava River by massive enemy barrage fire. Soon after, the Soviets counterattacked, setting off new and furious fighting that did not decrease in intensity until the afternoon, when both parties settled down to a tacit truce to catch their breath and gather the many wounded. The *Danmark* had taken heavy losses; the regiment's two battalions had lost around three hundred men killed, wounded and missing. *SS-Ostubaf.* Krügel ordered his men to return to their earlier positions and to assume a defensive posture against any further enemy attacks between Vaci and Erkes. In the afternoon of September 23, the *Norge* regiment was involved in an attack against Baldone, moving from the Dekmeri-Katlapji line, while the division's armored units attacked from the north.

German defensive position with an MG 42 machine gun on the Latvian front, 1944.

Column of German army *PzKpfw.IV Ausf. H* tanks.

Waffen-SS 75 mm antitank gun face a soviet attack.

The village of Blunavas fell quickly into the hands of the SS grenadiers, but their progress was halted soon after by a counterattack made by strong Soviet tank forces with infantry following them. For the first time, *Nordland* grenadiers faced Sherman tanks, furnished to the Soviets by the Western Allies. The 75mm antitank guns had to be brought into play to stop the enemy steel monsters. Furious fighting ensued that involved the SS units; among the first to fall to enemy fire was Norwegian *SS-Ostuf*. Thomas Peter Sandborg, commander of *11./Norge*, hit by a burst of enemy fire while he was leading his men in an attack. The attack continued on September 24, with the SS grenadiers able to gain some ground. *SS-Uscha*. Petrat of *10./Norge* was able to destroy a Stalin tank with a *Panzerfaust* at close range. Other Soviet tanks were knocked out the same way. *SS-Ostuf*. Dirks[5], commander of *10./Norge*, was badly wounded, while one of his platoon leaders, SS-*Hscha*. Stolz, was killed. Soviet resistance intensified and the SS grenadiers were again forced to assume defensive positions. On September 25, after having reorganized and still under constant Soviet artillery and mortar fire, the *Norge* regiment grenadiers resumed their attack, and around evening were deployed along the Dekmeri-Asenbergi line, localities situated two kilometers north of Baldone.

A *Waffen-SS* MG 42 preparing to fire.

A German soldier armed with a *Panzerschreck*.

SS-*Stubaf.* Martin Gürz.

The Knight's Cross for Martin Gürz

On September 26, the front was stable along the Vaci-Erkes line (*SS-Pz.Gren.Rgt.24 Danmark*) and the Dekmeri-Asenbergi line (*SS-Pz.Gren.Rgt.23 Norge*). To the east, contact had been made with *225.Infanterie-Division* and elements of *11.Infanterie-Division*. During the day, the Soviets had been able to break through in the *III./Norge* sector. The battalion commander, *SS-Hstuf.* Martin Gürz, counterattacked with all available men, falling at their head. The counterattack by Gürz was supported by *12./Norge*, led by *SS-Ostuf.* Ahlf[6]. Based on a proposal by *SS-Ostubaf.* Fritz Knöchlein, *SS-Hstuf.* Gürz was recommended to be posthumously awarded the Knight's Cross, which was officially conferred on October 23, 1944. Following is the text of the proposal: '*During the offensive battles southeast of Riga* between September 23 and 27, 1944, the regiment was ordered to eliminate the Soviet vanguards (consisting of infantry and tank formations) which had broken into the German lines, cutting them off from the rear area, and to close the gap that they had created in the front line. SS-Hauptsturmführer Gürz and his battalion had to bear the brunt of that offensive action. Because the attack had been interrupted by a strong enemy armored counterattack, Gürz moved forward to personally lead his men in the attack. Thanks to his example, the attack resumed, the breach was eliminated and the front line was restored. The action and exemplary courage of SS-Hauptsturmführer Gürz were determining in obtaining this victory, thanks to which the threat to Riga was finally eliminated. SS-Hauptsturmführer Gürz died as a hero the day after the attack (on 26.09.1944)'.

SS-Ostubaf. Fritz Knöchlein.

SS-Ostubaf. Helmut von Bockelberg (left) meeting *SS-Brigdf.* Joachim Ziegler.

New clashes in the Tukums area

During the night of September 26, the *Danmark* regiment was relieved by an army unit. The Norge abandoned its positions the following day. Due to the pressure of the German counterattack, the Soviets were forced to suspend their attack against Riga and shifted their efforts further to the west. Because of this, the withdrawal of the *Heeresgruppe Nord* forces through Riga and Tukums was able to be carried out safely. But in the meantime, the Soviets had assembled numerous forces to make new attacks against the area north of Doblen. *SS-Brigadeführer* Joachim Ziegler, the *Nordland* commander, was ordered to carry out the withdrawal to the south to intercept the furthest point of the Soviet forces that had advanced towards the sea. On September 28, 1944, both the *Norge* and *Danmark* regiments, along with reconstituted elements of the *Nederland* brigade (after the return of elements of *Kampfgruppe Wagner*) went on to occupy defensive positions prepared by the Latvian and German labor companies, north of Doblen. The Soviets began to hit the positions held by the Germanic volunteers with artillery beginning on September 30; this was followed by infantry attacks that were repulsed by the Germanic units. Between October 5 and 6, the *III.SS-Pz.Korps* units were ordered to move to the Autz sector.

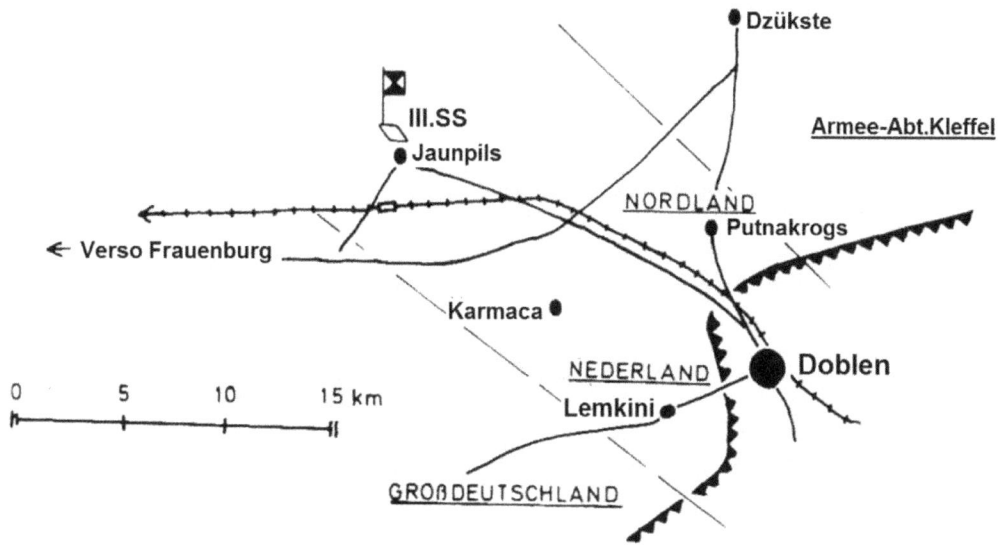

The new front at Doblen, September 28 – October 12, 1944.

SS-Ostubaf. Max Schäfer.

The *Nordland* headquarters was ordered to form a *Kampfgruppe* to send as soon as possible to the north of Moscheiken, where numerous Soviet forces had concentrated; the combat group, designated as *Sperrgruppe* (blocking group) *Schäfer*, named after its commander, SS-Ostubaf. Max Schäfer[7], consisted of both of the engineer battalions of the *Nordland* and *Nederland*, the *Nordland* recon group, the *III.SS-Pz.Korps* security company and a group of three artillery batteries from *Nederland*. These forces assumed positions in the Moscheiken area, between two *Wehrmacht* infantry divisions; the defensive line ran along the Vadakalis River, south of the hamlet of Roubas. On October 10, the Soviets attacked on the flanks in the sectors held by *Wehrmacht* units, overrunning them. The Soviet armored vanguards rapidly got behind the units of *Kampfgruppe Schäfer*; the grenadiers fell back to escape the enemy's grasp, covered by Dutch supporting artillery fire (*I./SS-Art.Rgt.54*) and by the armored vehicles of the *Nordland* reconnaissance group.

Notes

SS-Brigdf. **Jürgen Wagner**.

(1) Jürgen Wagner, born on 9 September 1901 in Strasburg in Alsace. After graduating in 1925 he joined the *Reichswehr*, which he left in 1929 to attend mechanical engineering studies. In March 1931, he joined the SS. On 20 April 1933, he was promoted to *SS-Sturmführer* and in July that year he was assigned to *SS-Sonderkommando Jüterborg*, a reserve and training unit for *Leibstandarte Adolf Hitler*, In October 1933, after being promoted to the rank of *SS-Sturmbannführer*, he took command of *II./LSSAH*, which he led until 1939. He then went first to the *Germania* regiment of the *SS-Verfügungstruppe* and then to *SS-Regiment 11* of the *Reich* division. In May 1942, he assumed command of the *Germania* regiment of the *Wiking*. On 11 December 1942, he was awarded the German Cross in gold. On 24 July 1943, he was awarded the Knight's Cross.

(2) Degrelle was born in 1906 in Bouillon, to a family of French origin. After having studied at the University of Louvain, he earned a doctorate in law. After having joined the Belgian Catholic Action, he soon became its leader. His books and his newspaper soon earned favor in public opinion and in 1936 his party earned 34 seats in the senate. That victory enabled him to meet personalities such as Hitler, Mussolini and Churchill, while at the same time being exposed to the influence of French nationalist Charles Maurras, Italian Fascism and of the German National Socialist Party. At the beginning of the war in 1939, Degrelle was arrested for his sympathies for Hitler's National Socialism and was imprisoned for some weeks until he was freed by the Germans. In 1941, following the Wallonian volunteer formation for the Eastern Front, Degrelle, 35 years old, married and with two children, volunteered, encouraging another thousand Walloons to follow his example. In February 1942, Degrelle participated with his Walloons in a bitter battle against the Soviets at Gromovaya-Balka, during which the Walloon formation suffered heavy casualties. For valor shown in battle, Degrelle was promoted to *lieutenant*. During the following summer and autumn, the Walloon volunteers were engaged in the Caucasus campaign, earning the esteem of German headquarters and of Himmler himself, who began to think about transferring the Walloons to his *Waffen SS*, which happened in summer 1943. With the *5.SS-Freiwilligen-Sturmbrigade 'Wallonien'*, in January 1944, Degrelle and his men were sent to the Cherkassy sector, subordinate to the SS-*Wiking* division. During the fighting against Soviet forces and after the death in combat of *SS-Sturmbannführer* Lucien Lippert, the Brigade commander, Degrelle was called upon to take command of the brigade. Coming out of Cherkassy alive, Degrelle was awarded the Knight's Cross by Hitler in person.

(3) Rolf Holzboog, born on 8 July 1914 in Stuttgart, SS-Nr. 32 263. He had served previously in *14./Sta. 'Deutschland'*, in *2./SS-Flak.Abt.5* and then in command of *4./Flak.Abt.11*.

(4) Albert Bergfeld, born on 27 August 1910 in Altena, SS-Nr. 16 034.He had served in command of *13./Nordland* and of *13.Danmark*.

(5) Meino Dirks, born on 5 March 1920 in Neudorf, SS-Nr. 309 889. He had served in *10./SS-Inf.Rgt.7*, in *15./Nordland* and in command of *10./Norge*.

(6) Hans Ahlf, born on 23 August 1914 in Neuhaus, SS-Nr. 202 367. He had served previously in *9./Sta. 'Germania'*, in *13./Norge*, as aide in *I./Norge* and in command of *10./Norge*.

(7) Max Schäfer, born on 17 January 1907. An SS engineer since its beginning, in June 1935 he was assigned to *2.Kompanie* of the *SS-VT* engineer battalion. In 1941 he was assigned to the *Wiking* division, first as a company commander and then as commander of the division's engineer battalion. On 12 February 1943, he was awarded the Knight's Cross, as *SS-Ostubaf.* and commander of *SS-Pionier Bataillon 5* of the *Wiking*. Later he took command of the engineers (*Kps.Pi.Fhr*) of *III.(germ.)SS-Pz.Korps*.

Bibliography

M. Afiero, "11.SS-Freiwilligen-Panzergrenadier-Division Nordland", Ass. Cult. Ritterkreuz

M. Afiero, "*The 11th SS-Freiwilligen-Panzergrenadier-Division Nordland*", Schiffer Publishing

The Italian Army in Russia
The Second Defensive Battle of the Don

by Massimiliano Afiero and Ralph Riccio

The Axis strategic situation on the Eastern Front in autumn 1942 appeared to be essentially static. After the rapid advances of the preceding months, the forces of Army Group B were bleeding themselves along the Don and in the area of Stalingrad and those of Army Group A were engaged in tough fighting in the Tuapse region on the River Terek. The situation of the 6th Army at Stalingrad under General Friedrich Paulus was especially critical. Likewise, the situation of the forces deployed along the course of the Don north and south of the city was worrisome in view of the winter season, not only because of the lack of reliability of the Italian, Romanian and Hungarian armies deployed in these positions, but also because of the presence of many Soviet bridgeheads on the western bank of the river, from which the Soviets would be able to mount counterattacks.

Alpini strongpoint on the Don front, autumn 1942. (USSME)

Already in August, during the so-called first defensive battle of the Don, the Italian forces had been forced to cede important positions on the right bank of the Don to the Soviets, at Serafimovich and Verhniy Mamon, while other bridgeheads had been taken by the Soviets at Kletskaya and Kremenskaya. After the difficult fighting in August, the Italian forces were shifted further north to the sector of the middle and upper Don, in September leaving the defense of the Serafimovich and Kletskaya sectors to the divisions of the Romanian 3rd Army, which had just arrived.

Soviet plans

While the Soviet 62nd Army under General Vasily Chuikov continued to hold on doggedly on the Volga, putting the German 6th Army to the test, the Soviet high command (the Stavka) was planning a series of counteroffensives, bearing the names of planets (*Uranus, Saturn, Mars* and *Jove*) to trap and destroy the Axis forces in the Stalingrad region and in the Caucasus as well as in the central region (Rzhev-Vyazma). The Soviet counteroffensive on the Stalingrad front was designated *Uranus*: the Southwest and Don fronts were to attack to the north and the next day, the Stalingrad Front was to attack to the south to eliminate the forces of the Romanian 3rd and 4th Armies. The pincer movement was to close at Kalach, surrounding Paulus' forces. Soon after, Operation Saturn would be launched against the Italian 8th Army, having as its final objective the destruction of Army Group B and the isolation of Army Group A in the Caucasus.

Defensive position being held by Black Shirts on the Don front, autumn 1942. (USSSME)

In the central sector of the front, General Zhukov had planned Operation *Mars*, with the Western and Kalinin Fronts engaged in eliminating the Rzhev salient, defended by *9.Armee*. Later, the Western Front would launch Operation *Jove* against *Heeresgruppe Mitte* in the Vyazma area.

The Axis Forces

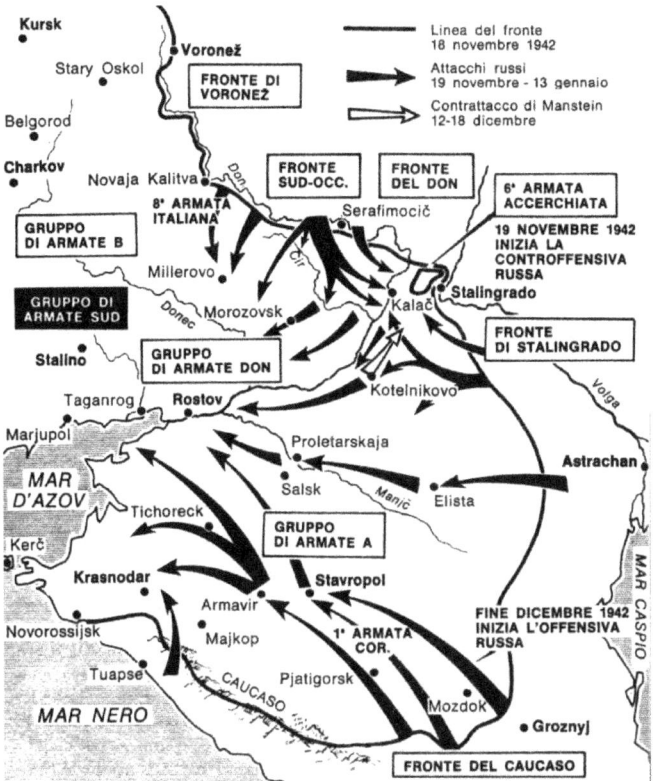

Italian 8th Army line deployments at the beginning of the Second Defensive Battle of the Don, autumn 1942.

BM-13 Katyuša rocket launchers open fire on Axis lines.

Soviet tank and infantry on the Stalingrad front, 1942.

The offensive begins

At 7:20 on 19 November 1942, the Soviets began a new offensive on the Don front, moving from their bridgeheads at Serafimovich and Kletskaya, preceded by artillery preparatory fire from 3,500 guns of varying caliber. However, because of dense fog, the Soviet artillery barrage did not produce the planned results and the Red Air Force was also forced to postpone its attacks to late morning. The infantry elements of the 5th Tank Army led by General Romanenko and of the 21st Army under General Chistyakov of the Southwest Front, attacked with tank support. The Romanian forces, after having overcome their initial surprise, reacted well enough, fighting as best they could. After having easily broken through the first defensive line, the Soviet soldiers in fact suffered heavy losses, thanks in part to the fire of the German-Romanian artillery batteries. But the superiority of the Soviet forces that had been fielded ultimately prevailed and both the Romanian 3rd Army led by General Dimitrescu and the Romanian 4th Army under General Constantinescu were completely overrun and on November 23, the forces of the Don front and Stalingrad made contact at Kalach, closing Paulus' *6.Armee* in a pocket.

Employment of the Italian units

On the Italian 8th Army front, not yet involved in the fighting, by order of Army Group B headquarters, the German divisions subordinate to the Italian Army were shifted to the sectors threatened by the Soviet offensive, in particular, *294.Infanterie-Division*, *22.Panzer-Division* and *62.Infanterie-Division*, thus depriving Italian 8th Army of its second-echelon divisions, the only forces which provided a minimum of depth along its 270 kilometer-long front. In addition, some Italian units also took part in the so-called Battle of the Volga. On November 22, men of the 2nd Reserve Regiment were placed in defense of Karginskaya to bar the road coming from Bokovskaya. During the night, a company of the II/54 of the '*Sforzesca*', reinforced with antitank guns, was moved to Chukarin to bar the valley of the Tchornaya.

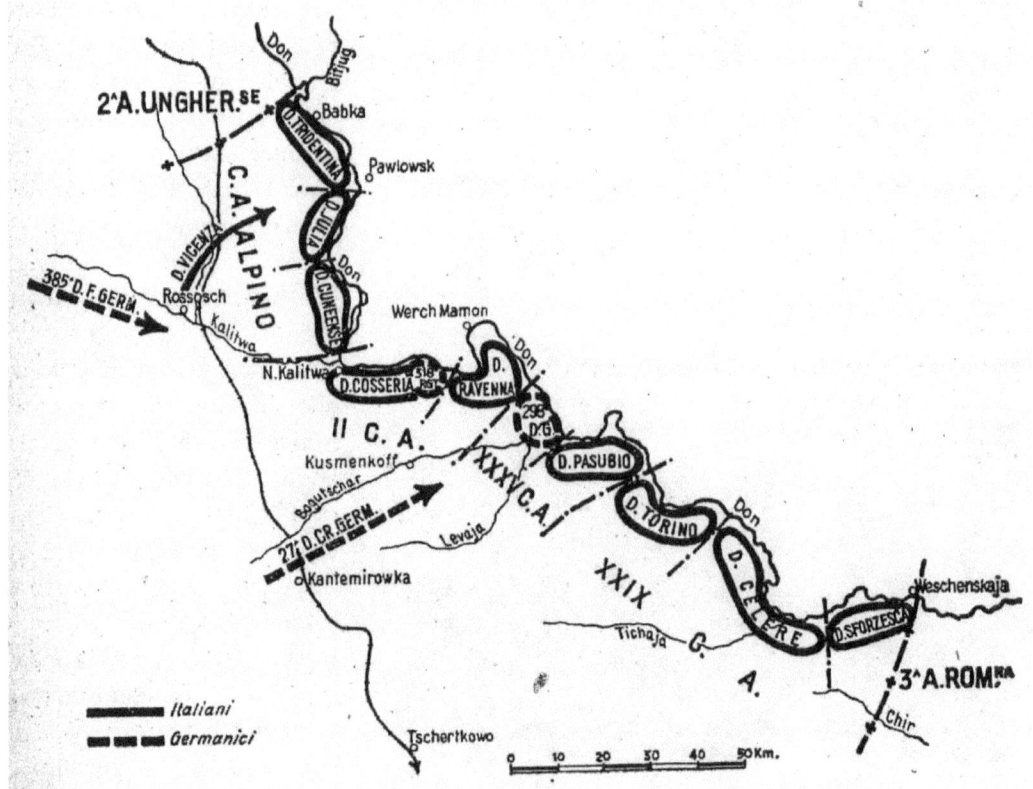

Italian 8th Army line deployment at the beginning of the Second Defensive Battle of Don.

On November 23, a reaction group from the '*Sforzesca*', led by General Michele Vaccaro, consisting of the headquarters and the 6th Company of the II/54, two companies of the CIV corps machine gun battalion, two 47/32 antitank companies and two 75/32 batteries of the I/201 were trucked into the sector to the right of the Romanian 9th division, which had been forced to withdraw to the right of the River Chir, at the confluence of the Tchiornaya at Bokovskaya. On 24 November, another reaction group arrived that had been sent by the '*Celere*', consisting of the LXVII L6/40 tank battalion, the XIII self-propelled 47/32 group and the XLVII Motorcycle Battalion, to protect the right flank of 8th Army. During that same day, the '*Sforzesca*' reaction group was engaged against a Soviet column headed from Otbeleize to Verhniy Gruskiy.

An Italian artillery battery ready to open fire, autumn 1942. (USSME)

Italian soldiers during an attack, December 1942. (USSME)

During the night of 25 November, the Soviets attacked the positions held by the Romanian 7th division, to the right of the '*Sforzesca*', calling Italian artillery into play and at the same time elements of the 54th Infantry were shifted to protect the division's right flank. Also on the 25th, the Vaccaro group's artillery supported a counterattack by *62.Infanterie-Division*, which had just arrived in the sector. On November 28, the Italian troops returned to the positions they had occupied earlier.

Italian soldiers on a defensive position, December 1942. (USSME)

An italian mortar in action, December 1942.

Trying to take cover

In the meantime, because of the presence of strong Soviet forces in the Boguciar sector and of Pavlovsk, 8th Army headquarters tried to bolster the corps front as best it could, transferring the 201st Motorized Artillery Regiment's headquarters and its III 75/32 group, attaching both units to the 'Cosseria' Division. The German headquarters, in that moment worried about reinforcing Army Group Don which was to attack from the southwest, across the Don, along the Kotelnikovo-Stalingrad line in an attempt to restore the continuity of the line between the Don and Stalingrad, but which was short of troops. It was not until the threat from the Boguciar sector loomed that the Germans decided to send in some reserves. On December 9, *Inf.Rgt.318*, commanded by *Oberst* Erich Mielke, a training unit which replaced the III/90 on the sector's right flank near the '*Ravenna*' positions in the Dereskova area, was transferred to the '*Cosseria*' division's front.

A Black Shirt machine gun team in a defensive position in the Verhniy Mamon bend, December 1942. (USSME)

A Black Shirt light machine gun squad during an attack.

Between 9 and 10 December, also arriving in the II Corps sector was *17.Panzer-Division* (consisting of a single tank battalion) which was deployed in the Kusmenkopf-Zapkovo-Krasni area, behind the line of contact between the *'Cosseria'* and the *'Ravenna'*, as well as three German antitank companies which were deployed in the *'Ravenna'* sector. The *385.Infanterie-Division* was also expected to arrive, moved from the Voronezh front. Facing the II Corps sector, where the Soviets had decided to make their main effort, were forces of two different fronts. In particular, the 6th Army of the Voronezh Front was deployed against the 'Cosseria' sector, while units of the 1st Guards Army of the Southwest Front were deployed against the sector held by the *'Ravenna'*. The Soviet forces totaled 90 rifle battalions, 25 motorized rifle battalions, 30 tank battalions (with 754 tanks), 2,065 artillery pieces and mortars, 300 antitank guns and 200 multiple rocket launchers. Facing these forces were the two Italian binary divisions (each with two infantry regiments rather than three) *'Cosseria'* and *'Ravenna'*, the *'23 Marzo'* raggruppamento (*'Tagliamento'* and *'Montebello'*), with 16 Italian infantry battalions, one sapper (XXX), 3 battalions of *Inf.Rgt.318*, 9 Italian batteries and about 50 panzers.

A Model 35 149/40 gun on the Don front, December 1942. The 149/40 was an excellent piece of artillery; all of these guns that were sent to Russia were lost to the Soviets. (USSME)

Italian *Breda* Model 37 machine gun. (USSME)

Early attacks

According to Soviet historiography, Operation Little Saturn against the Italian 8th Army began on 16 December 1942, when all of the units of the 1st Guards Army and of the 6th Army moved contemporaneously to attack the Italian II Corps. In Italian historiography, however, the same operation, designated as the Second Defensive Battle of the Don, began on December 11 when the first attacks by the Soviets began against the Italian defensive front, made to determine weak points against which the later general offensive would be mounted. These preliminary actions lasted five days, between 11 and 15 December.

The Axis Forces

Two 47/32 self-propelled guns of the XIII Gruppo *'Cavalleggeri di Alessandria'* on the move, December 1942. (from the book *'Dalla Russia noi siamo tornati'* by Attilio Scolari)

Black Shirts during an attack against an enemy position.

At dawn on 11 December, the first attacks against the II Corps front were made near the bend at Verhniy Mamon: at 6:40, after Soviet air attacks against the positions of the 38th Infantry, an attack by two infantry battalions of the 195th Rifle Division followed. At the same time, a battalion of the 128th Rifles attacked Hill 218 and a battalion of the 412th Rifles crossed the Don near the Svinyuka Plain. At 8:30, by request of II Corps headquarters, the Luftwaffe took action to hit the Soviet columns. In the afternoon the Soviets tried to bypass Krasno Orekovo and again attacked the strongpoint of Hill 218.0 near the Svinyuka Plain. The corps commander sent the two *'Valle Scrivia'* tactical groups to reinforce the *'Ravenna'*, to employ one in the Krasno Orekovo sector (I) and the other in the area of Hill 217.6 (II). The *'Leonessa II'* tactical group was sent to Svinyuka. The *'Cosseria'* positions were not attacked, but its artillery and mortars were committed to repel the enemy attacks.

Italian troops marching along a railways line, December 1942. (USSME).

Lieutenant Guido Cencetti.

In this early defensive fighting, Lieutenant Guido Cencetti of the 38th Infantry distinguished himself and was posthumously decorated with the Gold Medal for Military Valor, with the following citation: *"Magnificent figure of a fighter, a volunteer in three wars, full of passion and enthusiasm, bold and energetic arditi [elite assault troops] platoon leader, by word and example he heightened the daring of the infantrymen, hardened their spirit and with his unit, always first among the first, he faced every difficult mission. After the enemy had occupied an important position, he offered to recapture it with his platoon and leading it – heedless of all danger – he rushed into the attack with impetus and ardor. Wounded at the moment in which he was the first to break into the contested trench, he refused all aid and continued, by word and example to urge and push his men to action. Wounded a second time, mortally, he did not cease fighting until he actually died. In the last moments of life, turning his face towards the enemy, he pointed out the next target to his men and, so that he could see the enemy in flight and victory smiling on his platoon, he would not allow himself to be taken from the battlefield. A shining example of an intrepid, heroic soldier, a noble example of devotion to duty pushed to the supreme sacrifice. [Russian front – Don, 11 December 1942]"*.

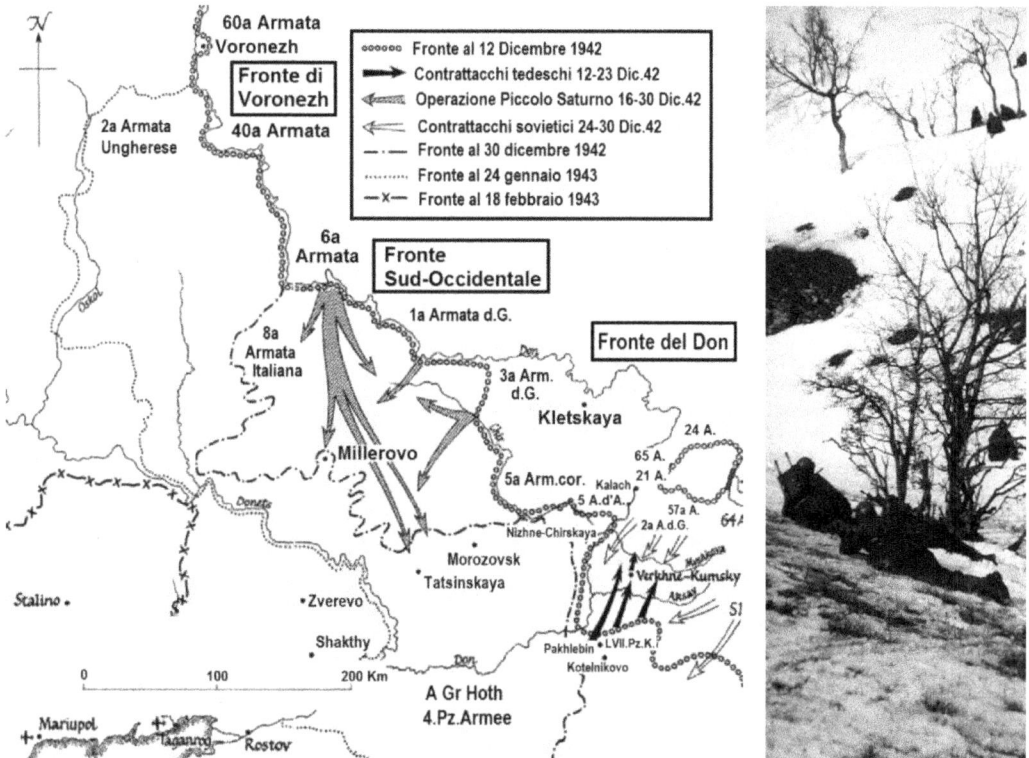

Left, operations on the Don front between December 1942 and February 1943. Right, Italian soldiers during an attack, December 1942.

Italian defensive position on the Don front, 1942.

On the XXXV Corps front, attacks were made against the 'Pasubio' front, near Ogalev, against the I/79 and then spread along the entire front held by the regiment. Thanks to action by the *'Tagliamento'* CC.NN. group and the XXX Battalion of the *'Montebello'* group, the attacks were repulsed. During the day, the division had received ten 75mm German antitank guns, one 88mm antiaircraft gun and two 20mm antiaircraft guns as reinforcements. On December 12, Army Group B headquarters, still unaware that the Soviets had chosen the II Corps sector for their main attack, planned to transfer the *387.Infanterie-Division* further to the north, at the juncture point between the Alpine Army Corps and the Hungarian 2nd Army. During the morning, the Soviets attacked with two infantry battalions in the *'Cosseria'* division's sector, between Novo Kalitva and Koschiarni, held by the II/89. Another two battalions attacked in the sector between Samodurovka and Dereskova, defended by the II/90. The situation was not restored until that night. On the *'Ravenna'* front, attacks continued against the strongpoints of Krasno Orekovo and Hill 218.0. In the afternoon, the 38th Infantry recaptured a strongpoint near Krasno Orekovo, while the 37th Infantry was busy warding off fresh enemy attacks at Svinyuka.

Italian soldiers on a defensive position on the Don front, December 1942. (USSME)

Italian soldiers during an attack, December 1942.

On the XXXV Corps front, the Soviets continued their attacks in the bend of the Ogalev against the length of the 79th Regiment's front. Throughout the day, Soviet attacks alternated with Italian counterattacks, mounted mainly by the *'Tagliamento'* group, by the VI CC.NN. Battalion and by two ad-hoc companies. Ogalev was completely levelled during the fighting. Arriving as reinforcement was the 3rd Division *'Celere'* reaction group (LXVII Armored Battalion with 31 L6/40 light tanks, XIII Squadron Group with 19 47/32 self-propelled guns and the XLVII Motorcycle Battalion) as well as all of the XV Sapper Battalion. Falling while leading his men was Centurione [Captain] Ettore di Pasquale of the VI *'Montebello'* truck-borne CC.NN. battalion, posthumously awarded the Gold Cross for Military Valor, with the following citation: *"A company commander of great ability and unlimited enthusiasm, he asked for and was allowed to participate in a difficult action. Despite the heavy enemy fire and over ground that was particularly difficult for an attack, he decisively led his company in an assault, directing every move under increasingly violent fire. Wounded, he refused any aid and, still leading his men, personally maneuvered the reserve detachment, leading it right up to the enemy positions and himself fighting hand-to-hand. Wounded a second and a third time by hand grenades, he continued stoically, despite his serious wounds, leading the attack with indomitable spirit, having his men hold him up. With a final supreme effort, at the head of his men, he reached the contested position on the Don, where a fourth wound cut short his heroic resistance. A magnificent example of absolute dedication to duty.* [Russian front, 12 December 1942]".

Centurione Ettore di Pasquale (movm.it).

Italian troops awaiting orders to move.

On December 13, along the II Corps front and especially against that of the '*Cosseria*', the Soviets attacked Nova Kalitva, engaging the II/89. To deal with them, the III/89 and the '*Cuneense*' alpine division's artillery had to rush to their aid. The Soviets made another attack against the eastern part of Samodurovka, held by the I/90 and was driven back. In the late morning, attacks against Hill 192 were resumed but were defeated thanks to the use of reserves from Orobinski. To reinforce the defenses, the Army headquarters granted the use of one battalion from 385.Inf.Div. which had been located in Zapkovo. Towards noon, almost all of Samodurovka fell into Soviet hands; only a few points of resistance continued to fight on. In the afternoon, enemy pressure also increased in the Novo Kalitva area. A counterattack was mounted against Samodurovka which brought the Italian units as far as the right bank of the Don and the Soviets were also thrown off of Hill 192.0. At Dereskova, *Inf.Rgt.318* repulsed an attack against the western side of the position. At the end of the day, *Grenadier-Regiment 537* entered into action, having been transferred to II Corps, which had already integrated the Italian forces engaged in the sector, namely the II and III/89. The counterattack led to recapture of several strongpoints and to the capture of large quantities of arms and ammunition.

Italian artillery on the Don front, December 1942. (USSME)

A German *Panzer* on the Don front, December 1942.

On the '*Ravenna*' front, the '*Valle Scrivia*' tactical group was sent in as a reinforcement in an attempt to restore the situation at Krasno Orekovo, which was still under enemy attack. The follow-on counterattack led to the recapture of two strongpoints that had been lost as well as to the isolation of enemy forces in several balkas. In order to repel any Soviet tank attacks, the transfer of a combat group of the *27.Panzer-Division* was requested, which included 16

75mm self-propelled guns, one infantry battalion and two heavy antitank companies, from Pereschepni to Gadyuche.

Withdrawal of Italian units, December 1942. (USSME)

Withdrawal of Italian units, December 1942. (USSME)

On the *'Pasubio'* division's front, reinforcement came in the form of a reaction group of the 298.Infanterie-Division to recapture Ogalev. As it had already in part been retaken by the *'Tagliamento'* group, then replaced by the XV Sapper Battalion, the division commander decided to keep only a German infantry battalion and its artillery as a reserve. On December 14, along the *'Cosseria'* division's front, a counterattack was made against Hill 192.0, using the *'Leonessa II'* group. It was not possible to have the tanks of *27.Pz.Div.* join the action because they were directly subordinate to the Army. However, the Soviets were nonetheless forced to withdraw. At the same time, an attack against *III./Inf.Rgt.318* was repulsed on the western side of Dereskova. Around noon, new fighting flared up on Hill 192.0, following an attack by two Soviet battalions. Once again, the *'Leonessa II'* tactical group was engaged.

Italian soldiers on a defensive position, December 1942.

Italian soldiers in a trench on the Don front.

Around 14:00, Hill 192.0 again fell into Italian hands, while at Dereskova, several positions held by *Inf.Rgt.318* had fallen. From prisoner interrogations it was learned that three Soviet divisions had been in action against the *'Cosseria'* but had suffered such heavy losses in the day's attacks that the 127th Rifle Division had to be disbanded. The *'Cosseria'* reported the loss of at least a thousand men killed, wounded and missing. In the *'Ravenna'* sector, attacks against Hill 218.0 had resumed at dawn, while arrival of large enemy forces were reported between Verhniy Mamon and the left bank of the Don. In the afternoon, the Soviets attacked the division's left wing in force near Krasno Orekovo, where all of the available reserves were thrown in. The strongpoints were doggedly defended and at 22:00, the *'Ravenna'* infantry mounted a counterattack which forced the Soviets to pull back. On the *'Pasubio'* front, at 6:00 the stretch defended by the III/79 was attacked. After about two hours of intense fighting and thanks to supporting fire by artillery and mortars, the attack was driven off. Other attacks were made against the II/79, with the Soviets attempting to push their lines forward.

An Italian soldier in a trench on the Don front, December 1942.

Italian mortar on a defensive position.

After four days of continuous attacks against the Italian positions, the Soviets had made an accurate assessment of the situation, identifying the weakest positions in the defensive line. Their actions had focused mainly against the II Corps front, while offensive actions against the 'Pasubio' had been made only as diversions.

New attacks, new dispositions

On December 15, General Italo Gariboldi requested that new urgent measures be taken by Army Group B, and especially for new reinforcements to lessen the constant enemy pressure. That same day, at 11:30, the 'Cosseria' launched a new counterattack against Hill 192.0, meeting stiff resistance and taking heavy losses. In the afternoon, the German liaison office reported to Italian II Corps headquarters that a battalion of *Grenadier-Regiment 539* had been transferred to the 'Cosseria' division to recapture Hill 192.0. In light of the counterattack on the following day, this battalion was resubordinated to *27.Pz.Div.* In the meantime, the II/90, the III/90 and the three battalions of the *'Leonessa'* group continued to fight around Hill 192.0. In addition, to bolster coordination between the I/90 and the area of Hill 192.0, ad hoc units from the rear area were moved up to the line.

Alpini of the *Monte Cervino* armed with MAB 38A submachine guns and a Model 91 carbine, before going into action on the Don front, December 1942.

General Italo Gariboldi.

At 20:15, 8th Army headquarters issued the dispositions received from *Heeresgruppe B*:

-385.Inf.Div., with all of its units present in the area, came under subordination of II Corps to restore the situation in the 'Cosseria' sector.

-The *'Cosseria'* Division, which during the night was to be replaced by *385.Inf.Div.*, was to have retired its infantry regiments, but was to leave the divisional and reinforcing artillery in place.

-The II Corps commander intended to use the *'Cosseria'* troops to support the *'Ravenna'*.

After five days of harsh and exhausting fighting, the Italian 8th Army forces had managed with great sacrifice to substantially hold their positions and General Gariboldi expressed his praise to the combatants : *'To the brave soldiers of II Corps. For five days you have been fighting strenuously and have gloriously earned your motto 'They shall not pass'. Bravo! I am proud of you. We have to hold out tenaciously, with unshakable faith and you will win, earning the admiration and recognition of our homeland'*.

Italian troops pulling back to a new position, December 1942. (USSME)

Italian bersaglieri on the Don front, 1942.

The Italians had held up well, but nonetheless the Soviets had been able to achieve their objective during this first phase of the battle, namely, to wear down the Italian forces to the point that they would be less capable during the next phase of the offensive. In five days, the Soviets had mounted a total of twenty-one attacks against the *'Cosseria'*, *'Ravenna'* and *'Pasubio'*, committing between 26 and 28 infantry battalions.

Operation Little Saturn

At dawn on 16 December, Soviet artillery, with over 2,500 guns of all calibers, opened fire on the Italian II Corps positions. Then the tank and infantry units attacked. The Italian forces, although exhausted by the fighting of the preceding days :

'...offered fierce resistance and often went on the counterattack. To effect the breakthrough of the tactical defense, it was necessary from the outset to commit the armored units. This fact led to the decrease of their combat capability in the later in-depth actions. At the end of the day, the 6th

Generale Enrico Gazzale.

General der Infanterie **Karl Eibl.**

Army forces had advanced four or five kilometers and those of the 1st Guards Army two or three kilometers', respectively against the *'Cosseria'* and the *'Ravenna'* divisions.

On the II Corps front, throughout the night, the Soviets had made numerous attacks to break through the lines of German *Inf.Rgt.318* and the Italian 38th Infantry. In order to ease the pressure, General Zanghieri ordered an attack by a German police battalion, supported by a company of L6/40 light tanks of the LXVII Bersaglieri Battalion. At 6:00, the *'Cosseria'* commander, General Gazzale, transferred operational responsibility of the sector to *General der Infanterie* Karl Eibl, commander of *385.Inf.Div.*. The two headquarters had remained at Krasni, to ensure salvaging the Italian units. At 8:00, the situation continued to worsen; Soviet troops had managed to break through the lines of *385.Inf.Div.* in several points and Dereskova had been abandoned by the Germans. At the same time, on Hill 192.0, the Italian attack supported by *27.Pz.Div.* tanks, was stopped by Soviet artillery and air strikes. Other enemy attacks developed against Samodurovka, where the I/90 was surrounded, while Soviet tanks had already made it to Gorohovka. Around noon, the Soviet attacks spread across all of the right-hand part of the sector, making it impossible to pull out any of the Italian troops. Army headquarters transferred *27.Pz.Div.* to II Corps in order to try to maintain contact between the various units.

In the *Ravenna* sector, beginning with the first light of dawn, Soviet tank units descended from Hill 193.6 and from Ossetrovka. The fire of all of the artillery in the sector was concentrated against them. At the same time, other attacks were made north of Krasno Orekovo, while all of the positions were subjected to massive Soviet artillery fire. To stop the Soviet tanks, *Kampfgruppe Maempel* was alerted, consisting of self-propelled guns and tank destroyers from *27.Pz.Div.*, led by *Major* Rolf Maempel, coming from Pereshchepnoye. At 7:00, two 38th Infantry strongpoints and one of *Inf.Rgt.318* were overwhelmed by enemy

The Axis Forces

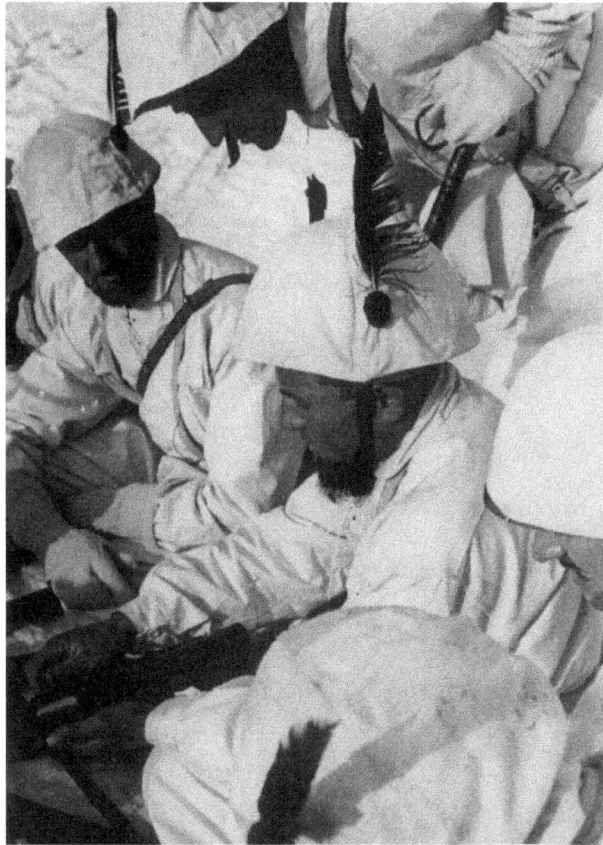

Soldiers of the *'Monte Cervino'* alpine ski battalion.

Italian soldiers marching in the snow, December 1942.

attacks. At 9:00 the positions on the western side of the bend of Verhniy Mamon were overrun and Soviet armored units reached the villages of Krasno Orekovo, Gadyucce and Filonovo. In an attempt to salvage the situation, the II Corps commander sent the LXVII armored battalion and the XIII self-propelled group to reinforce the *'Ravenna'*. The first wave of Soviet tanks, consisting of about fifty tanks, was almost completely destroyed by mine fields, artillery fire and by the self-propelled guns of *Kampfgruppe Maemel*. At 10:30, the *'Ravenna'* positions were again under attack by the 195th Rifle Division in the Krasno Orekovo area, where the defensive line had been penetrated and the various strongpoints were surrounded and eliminated one by one by Soviet tank units. On the western side of the bend at Krasno Orekovo, the 41st Guards Division attacked, following the road from Hill 193.6 to Hill 150.2, and to the east, the 44th Guards Division attacked around Hill 218. The **Italian soldiers marching in the snow, December 1942.**Soviet tanks eliminated the strongpoint held by a company of the CII Machine Gun Battalion, which until the very end had inflicted heavy losses on the enemy infantry with the fire from its twelve machine guns. General Francesco Dupont, commanding the *'Ravenna'*, decided to stabilize the new line of resistance on the positions at Hill 204.2, Hill 217.6, Hill 196.3 and Svinyuka, striking from the north against the villages of Gadyucce and Filonovo, committing the forces that were withdrawing. But around noon, the situation continued to become more critical, with the *'Ravenna'* positions hit by Soviet aircraft and with new tank attacks throughout the sector. General Zanghieri, in agreement with the German liaison officer, proposed shifting the defense along the Zapkovo-Orobinski-Dubovikov-Goly-Hill 179.2-Lufizkaya line in order to cover the Boguciar Valley. In the early afternoon the order was given by *Heeresgruppe B* that forbid any withdrawal; the '*Ravenna*' division was to hold its positions. At 17:00, the men of the division assumed positions along the line Hill 217.6-Filonovo-Gruscevo balka-Hill 159, where it linked up with *298.Inf.Div.*, deployed around its artillery pieces and the few German tanks. There were about three thousand men, exhausted after six days of fighting and without enough weapons and ammunition. Further exacerbating the situation were the violent bombardments by enemy multiple rocket launcher batteries and aviation. At 18:00, the Army headquarters informed II Corps headquarters that reinforcements in the form of elements of the '*Julia*' alpine division and the '*Monte Cervino*' alpine ski battalion would be arriving.

An Italian 20mm Breda Model 39 anti-aircraft gun on the Don front, December 1942. (USSME)

Italian soldiers marching in the snow, 1942.

Attacks against XXXV Corps

The attack against the '*Pasubio*' positions began at 6:00, without any artillery or rocket launcher preparatory fires, but supported mainly by mortar fire, especially in the Krassnogorodovka – Abrossimova -Monastirschina stretch. In late morning, between 9:00 and 10:00, troops of the Soviet 38th Guards Division breached the positions of the 80th Infantry southeast of Abrossimova, forcing the Italian soldiers to retreat. Abrossimova fell shortly afterwards and the attack continued towards hills 187.9 and 206.3, as well as further to the south, cutting off the Monastirschina Valley. The 1st Antitank Battery of the 1/201, with 75/32 guns, was completely wiped out while attempting to oppose the enemy advance. At the same time, the infantrymen of the II/80 and the gunners of a section of the I/201, through the Artykulny Schlucht Valley, fell back onto the batteries of the III/8, which were also under attack and forced to fire over open sights. Following the withdrawal of the infantrymen, the artillery observers also began to fall back, having to open a path while fighting. On Hill 206.3, the remnants of the III/80 continued to fight doggedly.

Alpini on a defensive position with a *Breda* machine gun, December 1942. (USSME)

Another photo of the Alpini defensive position.

The strongpoints in the bend of the Ogalev, were still experiencing frontal attacks. At strongpoint *Olimpo*, all of the defenders were killed by enemy fire. The Black Shirts of the '*Montebello*' group counterattacked the enemy forces on Hill 187.9, Hill 178.3 and Hill 175.1 overlooking the Artykulny Schlucht Valley. From Army headquarters came the order to support the '*Pasubio*' with *Grenadier-Regiment 526* (*298.Inf.Div.*) and with all of the available forces of XXIX.Armee-Korps. In the afternoon the *298.Inf.Div.* reaction group, consisting of a battalion from *Gren.Rgt.526* and a 150mm artillery group that was attached to *Gren.Rgt.525* already deployed between Hill 201.1 and Hill 156.0, were provided to *'Pasubio'* headquarters. Towards evening, the new *'Pasubio'* defensive line was laid out as follows: on the left was the 79th Infantry as far as the southern edge of Krasnohorovka, in the center, from Hill 156.0 to Hill 201.1, were the German units, and on the right, along the line held by the *'23 Marzo'* Black Shirts were the remaining men of the 80th Infantry and an ad hoc battalion consisting of skiers, carabinieri and headquarters personnel. The front between this last-named battalion and the village of Monastirchina was exposed. At Monastirchina the I/80 was still holding out, with its survivors holed up in the church. In late evening, arriving as reinforcements to XXXV Corps, sent by 8th Army headquarters, were a railway battalion, a bridging battalion and an engineer battalion, all of which were to be used as infantry.

Clashes on 17 December

During the night, the temperature dropped to 30 below zero, making conditions even more difficult for the soldiers who had to fight in the open. On the II Corps front, at 3:00 on 17 December, a new tank attack was made against Samodurovka and Dereskova, making the attempt to establish contact between *358.Inf.Div.* and the *'Ravenna'* even more difficult. After having reached the Italian artillery positions, Soviet tanks overran the 1st and 3rd batteries of the CXXII 149/13 group of the 2nd Raggruppamento.

Withdrawing Italian troops using mules to carry their heavy weapons, December 1942.
(USSME)

The new situation and considering the few available forces convinced the II Corps commander not to engage the *'Cosseria'* as the link between *385.Inf.Div.* and the *'Ravenna'*. A little before 9:00, infantry supported by tanks moved from Dubovikov towards

The Axis Forces

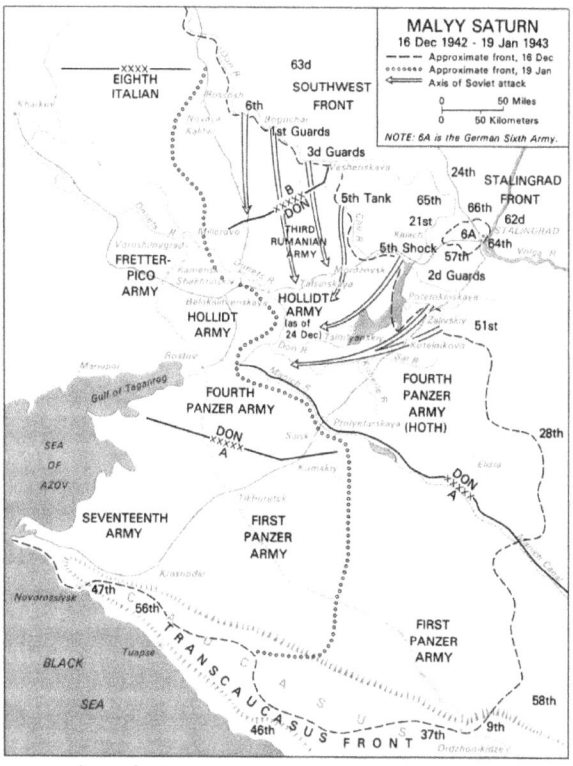

A column of T-34 tanks, December 1942.

German self-propelled assault guns attack.

Orobinski; facing them were only a few Italian 47mm guns and German 88mm guns. Especially threatened was Krasny, where three division headquarters were located (*385.Inf.Div.*, *'Cosseria'* and *27.Pz.Div.*). At 9:30, the *'Cosseria'* commander was ordered to establish, with the forces still available to him, a defensive front between Ivanovka and Kusmenkov. At 10:15. General Zanghieri informed the Army headquarters that following the fall of Orobinski and Zapkovo as well as the fall of Krasny, a new defensive front could be established along the line Novo Kalitva-Ivanovka-Kusmenkov or along the line Novo Kalitva - Dereskova - Kusmenkov. Meanwhile, II Corps headquarters moved from Taly to Mitrofanovka. Around 14:00, the Army chief of staff transmitted the orders of the German high command to General Zanghieri: at dusk, *385.Inf.Div.* and *298.Inf.Div.*, with the Italian forces attached to them, were to withdraw to the Novo Kalitva - Zapkovo-Tvyerdoklebovka – Lufizaya -Boguciar line, linking up on the left with the Alpine Army Corps and on the right with the *'Pasubio'* division, to form a solid front. On paper, everything seemed simple, but to form a solid front with men that had survived seven days of fighting without a break, with two reduced-strength German divisions and two Italian divisions at the end of their tether, represented a daunting challenge. In any case, at 20:00, the troops took positions along the new line, which began at the

An italian soldier in a trench on the Don front.

Don near Novo Kalitva, with two strongpoints held by the I/89, continued on to Hill 221 (southeast of Koschiarny)-Zapkovo-Sorky-Dolgy-Kusmenkov). Three German battalions were stationed on Hill 190 and at Zapkovo, elements of 27.Pz.Div. were at Sorky, Italian engineer forces and L6/40 tanks at Sorky and Dolgy. Between Dolgy and Kusmenkov was another open gap which was supposed to be occupied by the *'Monte Cervino'* battalion. Throughout the day, on Hill 192.0 the surviving men of the II and III/90, of the *'Leonessa'* group and of *III/Gren.Rgt.539* had continued to hold out, beating back continuous Soviet attacks. The breakthrough of Soviet tanks at Orobinski had isolated these troops. Therefore, the *385.Inf.Div.* commander had ordered their withdrawal after midnight, seeking to break the enemy encirclement. In the left-hand sector, the survivors of the I/90 pulled back to the support battery, which was left with only one gun, and then to that of the 3rd Battery of the I/108. After more defensive fighting, the men withdrew to Zapkovo, protected by the 3rd Mortar Company of the CV divisional battalion, which unleashed a desperate counterattack. The divisional artillery positions, attacked by Soviet tanks, defended themselves as best they could. The 2nd Battery of the CXXIII/2 held out until the night, but was then overwhelmed by Soviet infantry attacks. The 1st and 2nd 75/18 batteries of the I/108 met the same fate. However, the 2nd and 3rd 105/28 batteries of the IV/108 were able to withdraw while fighting, while the group's 1st Battery also was overrun. The fall of Hill 217.6, which dominated the villages of Gadyucce and Filonovo, made necessary a further withdrawal by the *'Ravenna'* troops to Sovkos Boguciarsky and Pereschepny. Not all of the units of the *'Ravenna'* had reached Gadyucce and Filonovo; about a thousand survivors of the 37th Infantry, after having run out of ammunition, continued their march until they reached Pereschepny and the *298.Inf.Div.* sector. At 9:30, when General Dupont reported to the corps headquarters, he was ordered to engage the forces present at Pereschepny to support *Kampfgruppe Maempel* and to establish a linkup position with *385.Inf.Div.* at Sovkos Boguciarsky. The remaining personnel of the division were to regroup at Tverdoklebovka to provide support to the two other groups and where the division's tactical headquarters had set itself up. At 10:30 General Manlio Capizzi, the *'Ravenna'* infantry commander, arrived in Pereschepny, assuming command of an Italian

The Axis Forces

Major **Rolf Maempel.**

Italian soldiers on the Don front.

group which included elements of the 37th infantry, which made contact with *298.Inf.Div.*. While awaiting the arrival of the *'Monte Cervino'*, the division was ordered to establish a defensive position at Kusmenkov, using the available men and equipment to block any enemy penetration in the Boguciar Valley and to the south. At the same time, *298.Inf.Div.*, which had been subordinated to II Corps, after having been reinforced with the Gruppo *Capizzi*, began to withdraw its left wing, to bear against Boguciar. However, instead of the German units deploying along the river, they withdrew further to the rear, along the course of the Levaya, leaving the way to Boguciar and the Levaya open to the Soviets and making it possible for the enemy to get around the right wing of the 8th Army, held by the XXXV Corps. The Soviet attacks against the *'Pasubio'* had resumed at dawn against the positions south of Krasnohorovka. Then, after 10:00, the positions held by the III/79 were attacked. An enemy breach on the II/79 front was eliminated by the railway battalion that had arrived the previous night. Also along the *XXIX.Armee-Korps* front, the Soviet troops which had crossed the Don during the attack against Monastirschina had extended their action to the south, capturing Hill 162.9, which dominated the entire left wing of the *'Torino'* division and in particular the positions of the III/81. The II/81, which had been engaged the previous day at Monastirschina, was thrown into a counterattack, but with no success. In order to restore the situation, the III/82, reinforced with a company from the CIV Machine Gun Battalion, was shifted from the right-hand sector to that on the left.

The situation of the 'Celere'

Following the defeat of the Romanian 3rd Army at the beginning of the Battle of the Volga, the *'Celere'* division, located in the second echelon in the valley of the Boguciar, was called upon to defend a stretch of the front about 50 kilometers long that was occupied by *62.Inf.Div.*. The *'Celere'*, reinforced by the Croat Legion, was thus deployed straddling the lower course of the Tihaya, between the *'Torino'* and the *'Sforzesca'*. Considering the width of the front to be defended, the division also received the XXVI Mortar Battalion from the *'Torino'*, a company from the CIV Machine Gun Battalion and the LXXII mixed army group as reinforcements.

The mobile elements of the 'Celere', especially the XLVII Motorcycle Battalion, the LXVII Armored Battalion and the XIII self-propelled group were moved to the XXXV and II Corps sectors.

Italian soldiers on a defensive position, December 1942. (USSME)

At 7:00 the division's positions were attacked at the juncture point between the VI and XIII battalions. After about an hour, the attack spread to the positions of VI Battalion, near the confluence of the Tihaya and the Don, where some Soviet forward elements had been able to break through towards Tihovskoy. Other enemy units aimed for Hill 163.3, threatening Mrykin-Konovalov. Meanwhile, the 7th Battery of the II/120 was overrun by the Soviets. At 10:00, the XIX Battalion counterattacked towards the mouth of the Tihaya, but without success. At 13:00, strong Soviet forces went around Tihovskoy from the south, forcing the XIX Battalion to withdraw to the west for about a kilometer and defending Balatschkov. There the 105th divisional engineer company and the German 45th Railway Engineer Battalion arrived. At 15:00, also arriving was the German XVI observation group, consisting of about 200 men, to try to stop the Soviet breakthrough into the Tihaya Valley. At 16:30, a fresh attack against Hill 163.3 threatened the 3rd Battery of the I/120 and the village of Mrykin, where the headquarters of the 120th Artillery had been surrounded.

(to be continued)

Bibliography
Massimilano Afiero & Ralph Riccio, "*Snow, Ice and Sacrifice. The Italian Army in Russia 1941-1943*", Helion & Company Limited

www.ingramcontent.com/pod-product-compliance
Lightning Source LLC
LaVergne TN
LVHW081452060526
838201LV00050BA/1776